An Introduction to Bilingual Development

MM Textbooks bring the subjects covered in our successful range of academic monographs to a student audience. The books in this series explore education and all aspects of language learning and use, as well as other topics of interest to students of these subjects. Written by experts in the field, the books are supervised by a team of world-leading scholars and evaluated by instructors before publication. Each text is student-focused, with suggestions for further reading and study questions leading to a deeper understanding of the subject.

MM Textbooks

Advisory Board:

Professor Colin Baker, *University of Wales, Bangor, UK*

Professor Viv Edwards, *University of Reading, Reading, UK*

Professor Ofelia García, *Columbia University, New York, USA*

Dr Aneta Pavlenko, *Temple University, Philadelphia, USA*

Professor David Singleton, *Trinity College, Dublin, Ireland*

Professor Terrence G. Wiley, *Arizona State University, Tempe, USA*

Full details of all the books in this series and of all our other publications can be found on http://www.multilingual-matters.com, or by writing to Multilingual Matters, St Nicholas House, 31–34 High Street, Bristol BS1 2AW, UK.

MM Textbooks
Consultant Editor: Professor Colin Baker

An Introduction to Bilingual Development

Annick De Houwer

MULTILINGUAL MATTERS
Bristol • Buffalo • Toronto

Library of Congress Cataloging in Publication Data
A catalog record for this book is available from the Library of Congress.

De Houwer, Annick.
An Introduction to Bilingual Development/Annick De Houwer.
MM Textbooks: 4
Includes bibliographical references and indexes.
1. Bilingualism in children. 2. Language acquisition. I. Title.
P115.2.D44 2009
404'.2083-dc22 2009009450

British Library Cataloguing in Publication Data
A catalogue entry for this book is available from the British Library.

ISBN-13: 978-1-84769-169-9 (hbk)
ISBN-13: 978-1-84769-168-2 (pbk)

Multilingual Matters
UK: St Nicholas House, 31–34 High Street, Bristol BS1 2AW, UK.
USA: UTP, 2250 Military Road, Tonawanda, NY 14150, USA.
Canada: UTP, 5201 Dufferin Street, North York, Ontario M3H 5T8, Canada.

The policy of Multilingual Matters/Channel View Publications is to use papers that are natural,
renewable and recyclable products, made from wood grown in sustainable forests. In the
manufacturing process of our books, and to further support our policy, preference is given to printers
that have FSC and PEFC Chain of Custody certification. The FSC and/or PEFC logos will appear on
those books where full certification has been granted to the printer concerned.

Typeset by Saxon Graphics Ltd, Derby
Printed and bound in Great Britain by MPG Books Ltd

Dedicated to my daughter, Susan. I saw many of my earlier insights into bilingual development confirmed and learned more about it as I was a participant observer in her bilingual acquisition process. But Susan taught me much more besides. I am deeply grateful for her joy and wisdom.

Contents

Acknowledgements

I thank Multilingual Matters for the fact that they initiated this book, and that they put their trust in me to write it. The cooperation has been just wonderful!

This book was written after I finished writing a much more comprehensive textbook on bilingual development called *Bilingual First Language Acquisition*. Without that basis it would have been much harder to write this 'little' book. I thank Multilingual Matters for supporting me in writing the other book, and for the many colleagues worldwide who helped me find relevant sources and who gave me feedback. Specifically for this book I want to thank Ruying Qi and Lut Lams for checking on the Mandarin examples.

Thank you, especially, to all the bilingual children I have studied over the years and to the bilingual families who let me into their lives. Without them, this book could not have been written.

Preface

Research on bilingual development in young children has become quite prominent in the last decade. I use the term bilingual development here as a synonym for Bilingual First Language Acquisition (BFLA), or the development of two languages from birth. For obvious reasons, the topic has been of interest to parents and teachers. More and more students have become interested as well, either just in order to learn more about it, or to start their own investigations. Students interested in BFLA are in different departments and programs, and have different overall specializations. The main ones are Psychology, Linguistics and Education. In addition, there are also students in Sociology and Communication Disorders with an interest in the topic.

At the same time that students' interest in the topic has been on the increase, BFLA has more and more become a subtopic in many advanced level courses on a variety of subjects. BFLA may be a topic in a sociolinguistically oriented course on Bilingualism. Or it may be taught as part of a psycholinguistically oriented course on Child Language Acquisition. In Education programs, bilingual development may be discussed in the framework of a course on Second Language Acquisition. In Speech and Hearing programs, bilingual acquisition is often discussed in a course on Comunication Disorders.

The readings for courses that have BFLA on their subject list often include a selection of key primary publications, as well as overview chapters published in handbooks. For instructors wishing to give their students a more in-depth and teaching-oriented coverage of bilingual development (as part of a course on a larger topic), however, there are no texts available. This textbook aims to fill that gap. It is mainly intended for use in combination with textbooks on Bilingualism (for Bilingualism courses), or with textbooks on First or Second Language Acquisition (for courses on Acquisition). For a textbook on BFLA in the framework of a course that just deals with Bilingual First Language Acquisition I refer the reader to the other book I recently published with Multilingual Matters. That is simply called *Bilingual First Language Acquisition* and is much more comprehensive than this book aims to be.

The fact that this book was primarily conceived as an introductory textbook does not mean it cannot be useful to readers outside of academia. Scientific jargon has been kept to a minimum, and any lay person who reads English and is interested in knowing more about bilingual children should be able to understand this book. An extensive glossary at the end will help to understand some terms that may need explanation.

The multidisciplinary interest in bilingual development reflects the fact that Bilingual First Language Acquisition should be studied from a variety of perspectives. Regardless of one's particular perspective or research question, however, a real understanding of BFLA requires at least some background in two distinct areas of specialization: the field of child language development and the field of bilingualism. This book combines insights from both of these and thereby hopes to offer a richer perspective than either of these fields alone can offer.

Some technical notes about this book

- Children's ages are indicated in months or in years;months. For instance, 2;3 means two years and three months.

- I refer to CHILDES (Child Language Data Exchange System) in Chapter 1. This is a computerized archive that contains hundreds of transcripts of recorded conversations between children and other people (MacWhinney, 2000). There are also many transcripts available of conversations involving bilingual children. Anyone in the world can access this archive through http://childes.psy.cmu.edu/.

- Some of the specific children that I refer to are real children. I indicate this by adding a source. The four BFLA children whose individual language development I trace throughout the book are fictional, but are inspired by the many real children I know from firsthand experience and/or through the scientific literature. In talking about four fictional children, I follow up on many presentations I have given since 1993, including a keynote lecture I presented at a child language conference in 2002.

- When I talk about people in general, I use the plural. Gender indications refer to specific individuals only.

- Terms in the text that are marked in **bold** can be found in the glossary.

- Citations within the text are kept to a minimum in order to increase legibility. Key references that the preceding chapter draws on are listed at the end of each chapter.

- Chapters 1 to 4 are approximately the same length and can each serve as the basis for a class. Chapters 5 and 6 together are just a little longer than each of the preceding chapters and thus can together form the basis for a class.

1

Introducing the fancy term for bilingual development: Bilingual First Language Acquisition

This chapter sets the scene for the rest of the book.

- It defines the topic of this book. The topic is bilingual development, but as of now I will mostly use the more technical term for it, namely Bilingual First Language Acquisition or BFLA for short.

- It establishes that when children start hearing two languages from birth this usually happens within the family.

- It gives an introductory overview of BFLA children's major linguistic developments.

- It discusses the great range of variation that exists among BFLA children (and monolingual ones) during the ages at which major linguistic developments take place.

- It explains how BFLA children's two languages do not necessarily develop at the same rate.

- It emphasizes the role of the people that BFLA children interact with in helping to explain children's selection of one language rather than another.

- And, finally, this chapter introduces four BFLA children and their families whose bilingual development will be traced throughout most of the rest of this book.

What is Bilingual First Language Acquisition (BFLA)?

Bilingual First Language Acquisition (BFLA) is the development of language in young children who hear two languages spoken to them from birth. BFLA children are learning two first languages. There is no chronological difference between the two languages in terms of when the children started to hear them. This is why in referring to these languages it is best to use a notation that does not imply a notion of 'first' and 'second'. Following Wölck (1987/88) I will refer to BFLA children's two languages as Language A and Language Alpha.

I will be using the term Bilingual First Language Acquisition as a synonym for bilingual development. The term Bilingual First Language Acquisition is just more technical and precise.

My focus in this book is on children under the age of six. There are two main reasons: first, this book wants to describe how children become bilingual the way other children become monolingual, that is, without anyone formally teaching them. Children under the age of six typically learn language without formal instruction. This may change as they start to go to school around the age of six. Second, most of the scientific publications on bilingual development concern children under the age of six.

The definition of BFLA refers only to the *context* in which young children learn to speak. It differs from Monolingual First Language Acquisition (MFLA), in which children hear just one language from birth (their Language 1). BFLA also represents a different language learning context than Early Second Language Acquisition (ESLA), where MFLA children's language environments change in such a way that they start to hear a second language (Language 2) with some regularity over and above their Language 1. Often, this happens through day care or preschool. The BFLA context also differs from that of **Trilingual First Language Acquisition (TFLA)** where young children hear three languages from birth (e.g. Barnes, 2006).

BFLA, MFLA, ESLA and TFLA, then, are four different contexts for language learning in early childhood. Whether these different contexts all imply different language acquisition processes and developments is an issue that is beyond the scope of this book. However, I will, at times, draw comparisons between BFLA on the one hand, and MFLA on the other.

This book only talks about contexts where young children are hearing spoken language(s). Some children, though, may have little access to spoken language or it may even be absent. This is the case when children are born into families where the people taking care of them do not speak, but use sign language, or when children have a serious hearing loss that prevents them from hearing speech. If children growing up in these circumstances see two different sign languages from birth they may also be acquiring two first languages. Once there are studies documenting such contexts we may have to expand the definition of BFLA to include these as well.

The family as the primary setting for bilingual development

If children hear two languages spoken to them from birth, they will most likely hear them within the (extended) family. As such, the family is the primary setting in which children develop bilingually. There are, of course, many different kinds of families, and children grow up in many different kinds of family settings. When in the following I speak of 'parents' and 'couples' I am referring to all the people who take care of young children on a day-to-day basis. A single parent who has no help from others with a newborn baby may also create a BFLA situation by addressing the child in two languages from the very start.

Becoming a bilingual family   Two examples

From bilingual couple to bilingual family

Monika and Arnau have been married for two years. They were both raised in Spanish and Catalan, and use Spanish and Catalan between each other. Their relatives speak Spanish and Catalan every day as well. When their twin boys are born, Monika and Arnau continue to speak Spanish and Catalan at home between each other, and to their newborn babies. This feels the most natural and normal to them.

From monolingual couple to bilingual family

Ayhan and Marc speak English together. Ayhan is Turkish and Marc British. Marc understands some Turkish, but does not speak it. His family speaks only English. Ayhan's family only speaks Turkish. Ayhan herself is fluent in English. When Marc and Ayhan's baby girl Aylin is born, Turkish enters their home when Ayhan finds she simply cannot address the baby in English – it feels too strange and 'disconnected'. After a long conversation, Ayhan and Marc decide that Marc will speak to Aylin in English, and Ayhan will talk to her in Turkish. Marc will try to learn more Turkish so that he'll understand what's going on, and Marc and Ayhan decide that if Marc feels left out once Aylin gets a bit bigger, Ayhan could still use English when Marc is around, and switch back to Turkish when he's not.

The typical BFLA situation is the one where a newborn child's parents speak each of two languages when the baby is present. The chances are that during pregnancy, the not-yet-born infant heard mother speak two languages (that's right, infants can hear before they are born – see Chapter 2). But it is just as possible that until the birth the not-yet-born child's mother spoke only one language, and that the birth of the child triggers a change in the mother's language use.

Indeed, childless monolingual couples often become instant bilingual families upon the birth of their first child. This is most often the case when children are born to couples where the partners have different language backgrounds but speak only one language between themselves. After the birth of the baby one of them then starts speaking another language to the infant, and continues using the other language in addressing the other parent. Such changes in home language use patterns can have profound effects on the couple's relationship.

Alternatively, parents-to-be may both be bilingual and speak two languages at home. When the baby arrives, this pattern is just continued. There are also situations where bilingual couples decide to address their infant in just one language, thereby effectively blocking the possibility of BFLA. At the other end of the spectrum, monolingual parents may hire a nanny or 'au pair' out of the desire to raise their child with two languages from the very beginning.

It depends very much, then, on whether parents start speaking two languages to their baby as to whether a child will be raised in a BFLA setting or not. For some parents, it is a conscious decision to raise their child with two languages. For many others, speaking two languages at home is just a matter of course and not a matter of choice, very much the way that it is not a real 'choice' for completely monolingual parents to address their newborn child in the single language they happen to know and live with.

Developing in two languages from birth: An outline

Children who hear two languages from birth do not say much in the first year of life. Through **interactions** with people who talk to them regularly they do learn to *understand* **words** and phrases in two languages by their first birthday. This **comprehension** of language grows and grows, and never stops (at least not in healthy, hearing individuals).

After they are six months old, bilingual infants start to **babble**. This babbling lays the foundation for speech. Then, after their first birthday, bilingual infants start to say things that sound like words. At first, these are mainly single words. Some BFLA children may try to say longer things, but although the melodies of these longer **utterances** might sound like **sentences** it is impossible to make much sense of them. As bilingual children start to say more and more 'real' words, their babbling all but disappears.

Around their second birthday, bilingual toddlers speak in longer utterances. These now often consist of two or three words. Between two and three, BFLA children's language **production** really takes off, with many of their utterances now consisting of four, five, six or more words that are fully fledged sentences. From then on, the sky is the limit, and it is often difficult to keep bilingual children quiet!

Milestones in bilingual language development

The steps I've sketched above are very important in BFLA children's language development. They are so important that they are often called 'milestones'.

Milestones in BFLA children's early language development	
When? (roughly)	**What?**
between 6 months and age 1	babbling in syllables
by age 1	understanding many words and phrases in each of two languages
soon after age 1	saying what sounds like single words in one or two languages
between 1;6 and 2	noticeable increase in the number of different words BFLA children say
around age 2	saying two words in one breath
between 2;6 and 3	saying short sentences that have many of the little bits that adults would use
around age 3;6	BFLA children are mostly understandable to unfamiliar adults who speak the same language(s)
around age 4	saying sentences that consist of different clauses
between 4;6 and 5	ability to tell a short story that hangs together

The last age indication in the milestones box coincides with BFLA children's fifth birthday. There is still a lot to learn after age five, though (Berman, 2004). The very fact that no adult wants to sound like a five-year-old in any language is clear evidence of that. Not only do BFLA children learn a lot more words, idioms and phrases after age five, they also learn to construct more and more complex stories and become better conversationalists. They may also learn to read and write.

There is a particular order in overall language development that all young children follow. Babbling occurs prior to saying sentences, for instance, and comprehension precedes production. This is true both for BFLA and MFLA children (some of whom may become ESLA children).

Also the overall time frame in which the major developments in language take place is similar across young MFLA, ESLA and BFLA children. It takes about five years to develop enough language skill to tell a good story.

Normal variation in bilingual language development

In spite of the rather fixed order and the overall time frame of five years in which important linguistic milestones are reached there is a wide variation in the ages at which children reach them. This variation exists in both monolingual and bilingual children.

Let us take a closer look at the timing of important milestones. It might not seem much of a difference from the perspective of an adult life, but a difference of six months in the life of a two-year-old is quite a large difference: Six months in the life of a two-year-old means a quarter of her or his lifetime. But the six months between 18 and 24 months of age are the normal age range in which children *may* have reached the word combination milestone. Some children will be saying two-word combinations when they are one and a half, while others will be ready only at the time of their second birthday. Both possibilities represent the 'normal' variation, that is, the variation that occurs between children that you don't have to worry about. This normal variation is the same for MFLA and BFLA children.

If children miss some of the milestones, or if they reach them at a much later age than the rough age indications in the milestones box, something is wrong. Perhaps the children exhibiting these delays have a recurrent hearing problem, or there is an undiagnosed neurophysiological or psychosocial problem.

However, people often worry that all children who hear two languages reach the milestones much later than children who hear just one language. In other words, many people think that hearing two languages delays children's language development.

There is no research evidence showing that as a group BFLA children develop language slower than MFLA children. Instead, the combined evidence shows similar ranges of variation, with some BFLA children developing faster than some MFLA children, some MFLA children developing faster than some BFLA children, some BFLA children developing faster than other BFLA children, and some MFLA children developing faster than other MFLA children.

Hearing two languages, then, is not a danger to the language acquisition process. However, professionals who believe that it is and who deal with bilingual children can be quite harmful to them. The greatest danger exists if pediatricians or speech therapists fail to recognize or examine real underlying problems, such as hearing deficits, but instead blame the bilingual context for clear delays in language development.

What the belief that bilingual children develop more slowly can lead to

This pediatrician thinks that bilingual input leads to language delay. Therefore, she is not surprised to see a bilingually reared two-year-old who does not speak at all yet. She sees no need for a detailed examination and sends the father away with the advice to drop the minority language. She tells the father that all will soon be fine.

But after a year the child is back, and still does not speak. Upon examination (finally!), the child is found to be profoundly deaf. Most likely, the child's hearing was not good at age two, either. In this case, the doctor's prejudice has sadly resulted in lack of proper care for this young child.

There is also an idea that the 'solution' for children not learning to speak well in a bilingual setting is to drop one of the languages (see the box with the pediatrician). Apart from the fact that problems such as hearing loss do not go away if parents switch from a bilingual to a monolingual context, it is simply unethical to advise people to give up speaking a particular language and thus prevent them from transmitting much of their cultural heritage to their children. Negative attitudes towards child bilingualism, then, can prevent children from developing two languages in a stress-free way.

Varying levels of development in each language

People often assume that BFLA children know each of their languages equally well. This is not always the case, though. When we look at children's skills in a language we need to distinguish between comprehension and production.

BFLA children may understand many more words and phrases in Language A than in Language Alpha. Or they may understand sentences more easily in Language A than in Language Alpha. However, because of the small number of studies on comprehension in BFLA children we don't really know just how large these differences can be and whether it is possible for children to understand very little of one language but a whole lot of another, even though they have heard both of them frequently and regularly from birth. What little empirical research is available, however, suggests that there is a lot of variation between children in how many words they understand in each of their languages. I write more about this in Chapter 2.

For language production or speaking, there is ample evidence for large differences between BFLA children's two languages: there are children who do not speak Language Alpha at all but who are fluent in Language A. At the other end of the spectrum there are children who are about equally fluent in Language A and Language Alpha, and then there are all the variations between these two extremes, with children speaking one language better than the other to various degrees.

It is not easy to measure differences in how well children speak a particular language. Yet it is clear that BFLA children who speak two languages do not necessarily speak them equally well. A possible reason for this may be that children do not hear each of their languages to the same extent. I discuss the issue of variable knowledge and the possible reasons for it throughout the book.

Both these cases where BFLA children learn to understand two languages and speak either two or just one are quite 'normal'. In every fourth family where children hear two languages they speak only one. The fact that some BFLA children speak only one language, then, doesn't necessarily imply that they have a language learning problem. 'Il rigazzo' in the Case studies box below spoke Italian very well.

If BFLA children do not learn to understand and/or speak either of the languages spoken to them, this is cause for concern: maybe they have a hearing problem, or maybe there are neurological problems. Just as for MFLA children who do not understand much language and/or do not speak, the lack of comprehension and/or speech in any language in BFLA children is a severe problem and needs to be discussed with a speech and language pathologist.

Two case studies   Two normally developing BFLA children

An example of the more frequent case

Carlo was born to an American father and an Italian mother living in Scotland. For the first five months of his life, Carlo's father addressed him in English and his mother spoke Italian to him, as did his older brother. When Carlo was five months old he started to attend a half-day English-speaking day-care center on weekdays and his father started to address him in Italian rather than English. He continued to hear Italian from his mother and brother. Carlo also had Italian-speaking care providers on weekdays when he was not in the English-speaking day-care center. His parents spoke to each other in English.

Carlo grew up to understand and speak both English and Italian (Serratrice, 2001, 2002).

An example of the less frequent case

'Il ragazzo' (the boy) is the son of linguist Walburga von Raffler-Engel. He grew up in Florence, Italy. His mother always addressed him in Italian while his American father always spoke to him in English. Between each other, the parents spoke English. The child's broader environment was almost exclusively Italian-speaking. 'Il ragazzo' understood both English and Italian, but spoke only Italian: 'Il suo desiderio di perfezionarsi nell'inglese è quasi nullo' (Von Raffler-Engel, 1965: 176: his desire to speak English is just about zero – my translation). This doesn't surprise Von Raffler-Engel, since in her circle of acquaintants with lots of other Italian–American bilingual families it was very common for the children to speak just Italian, and no English, in spite of one of their parents addressing them in English.

The expectation for normally developing BFLA children, then, is that they will learn to understand two languages from early on and speak both languages, or just one of them.

Negotiating language choice in conversations

You'll be wondering how that works, children who are talked to in two languages but who speak only one? The answer is that people can be bilingual or monolingual, but conversations can be **dilingual** (Saville-Troike, 1987). For BFLA, this means that one person speaks in Language A, and the other one responds in Language Alpha. For dilingual conversations to work, the people engaged in them obviously must *understand* the two languages involved. However, in dilingual conversations there is no need for the conversational partners to actually speak the other one's language.

Case study   A dilingual conversation

Manuel (age: 2;1) hears German from his mother, who understands a bit of Italian. He hears Italian from his father. The family has two dogs, Poldo and Camilla. Manuel gives them some dog biscuits to eat. His mother is asking him about this. She speaks German and Manuel answers in Italian.

Mother: was hast du ihnen zu essen gegeben, Poldo und Camilla? haben sie etwas gegessen?

German for: what did you give Poldo and Camilla to eat? did they eat something?

Manuel: si.   *Italian for:*   yes

Mother: was denn?   *German for:*   what was it then?

Manuel: si.   *Italian for:*   yes

Mother: was? die?   *German for:*   what? those?

Manuel: bito.   *Italian for:*   biscuit

Manuel's 'bito' is a child version of the Italian word 'biscotto'

Mother: die bito.

Mother here repeats Manuel's Italian 'bito' and puts a German article in front of it. She then says in German: Kekse haben sie gegessen. (They ate biscuits)

Source: Klammler corpus, adapted excerpt from file germ5.cha, CHILDES

You'll have noticed that in the example from Manuel his mother in the end repeats his Italian rendering of 'biscuits', but translates it into German ('Kekse'). In doing so, she is acknowledging that Manuel said the right content, but in a form (Italian) that she'd like him to change (German).

In using such strategies as translating children's words into the other language, adults are expressing what language they want children to use. They are, in fact, negotiating children's **language choice**. This means they are trying to get children to select one particular language rather than another one.

Adults who try to get children to stick to just one language in a conversation are using **monolingual discourse strategies**. Monolingual adults won't have any choice here. If children talk to them in a language they do not understand, they'll be asking 'What?', which may result in children switching to the other language. Bilingual adults can also use this monolingual discourse strategy, even though they might have understood the child.

Bilingual adults who do not really care much about which language children speak to them won't make much of an effort to get children to speak just one particular language. They may have dilingual conversations with children all the time. Allowing such conversations is an example of <u>bilingual discourse strategies</u>.

Case study Switching languages in function of the setting

The girl Kate who was the subject of my case study on early English–Dutch bilingual acquisition was used to speaking Dutch with me. She also went to an English-speaking preschool, which was located in Antwerp, Belgium, where the main language is Dutch.

In the year after I had finished recording her for my study, when Kate was four years old, I got a part-time job teaching music at her English preschool. Of course, I had to speak English in the school, too. In this small international school, there was no room for Dutch. It was a little English-speaking island. All the children and staff were expected to speak English, regardless of their background. Kate happened to be in my class, so I spoke English to her there and she spoke English to me.

The school was right around the corner from Kate's house and Kate's mother had asked me if I could take her home after school. I still remember how I was escorting Kate from the classroom to the school's front door and how she was chattering away to me in English.

Then, I opened the door, we stepped down two steps onto the sidewalk, and she changed into Dutch! And I switched with her – I don't know how she would have reacted had I continued to speak English. But Kate obviously perceived the setting as very different, and switched back to what she had been used to with me from the time she was two years old: Dutch.

Children who interact with monolingual adults who speak Language A and with bilingual adults who speak Language Alpha with them but who allow children to respond in Language A have no communicative need to speak two languages and may end up speaking just one. Alternatively, children who are expected to respond in the language they are spoken to, whether it is Language A or Language Alpha, will learn to speak these two languages from early on and will switch between them when necessary – for instance, when the setting changes or when they are talking to a different person.

Introducing four bilingual families

In the next four chapters I will be tracing the bilingual development of four children in four families. I will follow these children from the time they are born until they are about six years of age. All the children are firstborn.

Lily

Lily is the daughter of Dutch Hein and Chinese Xiu. Hein met Xiu when he was on a business trip in China. Xiu was working at the Dutch embassy in Beijing and knows quite a bit of Dutch. They fell in love. Xiu agreed to marry Hein and come and live with him in the Netherlands on the condition that she and any children would be able to travel to China at least once a year to spend time with her family and friends.

From the time Lily was born, Hein and Xiu decided that they would each speak their respective language to her, namely Dutch and Mandarin. Xiu's Dutch is getting better and better all the time, and Hein understands a little bit of Mandarin. He is willing to learn more, but since he has a busy work schedule that won't be easy. Between each other, Xiu and Hein speak Dutch.

Arno

Arno is born to a French mother, Alix, and a German father, Bruno. The family lives in France, close to the German border, and both Alix and Bruno speak German and French fluently. Together, they speak either language depending on where they are and what they are talking about. They travel to Germany frequently, and Bruno's brother and children come and visit regularly. Alix and Bruno did not discuss what language they would speak to Arno but they happened to both start speaking to him in both languages pretty much from the start. You'll hear more about this in Chapter 2.

Ramon

Ramon is the son of Mexican-American Julia and Anglo–American Alan. The family lives in New Mexico in the United States of America. Julia is a fluent Spanish–English bilingual, and Alan speaks only English but understands some Spanish. Alan and Julia both speak English to Ramon when they are all together, but when Alan is not at home, Julia speaks Spanish to her baby. Julia's mother Rosa lives close by, and also speaks Spanish to Ramon, although she uses a lot of English words in her Spanish sentences. Rosa understands English fairly well, but doesn't really speak it other than that she borrows words from English in Spanish.

Toshie

Toshie has a Japanese father, Atsuo, and a Korean mother, Yun. The family lives in Japan and shares a house with Atsuo's parents. Atsuo and his parents only know Japanese, but Yun is fluently bilingual in both Korean and Japanese. She has lived in Japan for a long time and no longer has contact with friends or family in Korea. Yet she would like Toshie to learn to speak Korean. Atsuo agreed to this out of respect for Yun's heritage, but he is worried that when Toshie and Yun speak in Korean together he will be left out. Yun therefore plans to switch to Japanese in speaking to Toshie once she is old enough to talk and Atsuo is present. For now, though, Yun speaks only Korean to Toshie, since she has heard that children learn two languages most easily if each person speaks to them in just a single language. Yun continues to speak Japanese to Atsuo and his parents, of course, even though Toshie is present. You'll hear more about this in Chapter 2.

The Overview box summarizes the linguistic settings for the four BFLA children I introduced in this section. I also indicate which of the languages the children hear are used in public life in the place where they were born. This is called the **majority language**. The other language is called the **minority language**.

Remember, though, that some of the children will be travelling quite a lot, and thus the initial majority language does not necessarily stay the same. The Overview box also shows that there isn't always a single majority language. Two (or more) languages may play an important role in public life. Such is the case for bilingual cities such as Montreal (Canada) and Brussels (Belgium), for instance, and bilingual regions such as the southwest of the United States and the state of Gujarat in India.

Overview box Four BFLA children's language environments at birth				
Child	**Mother speaks...**	**Father speaks...**	**Other caregivers speak...**	**Majority language**
Lily	Mandarin and Dutch	Dutch	Mandarin or Dutch	Dutch
Arno	French and German	French and German	French and German	French
Ramon	Spanish and English	English	Spanish with English	English and Spanish
Toshie	Korean and Japanese	Japanese	Japanese	Japanese

You will have noticed that even though some of the bilingual parents in the four families have decided to follow what is called the 'one person, one language' principle (1P/1L), their children will still overhear them talking another language. This is the case for Lily and Toshie's mothers, who have started to speak Language Alpha when they are directly addressing their babies (respectively Mandarin and Korean), but who switch to Language A (Dutch and Japanese) when they talk to other adults, even when the baby is present. Indeed, the 1P/1L situation is usually an idealization. BFLA children growing up in a so-called 1P/1L situation will usually hear at least one person in their environment alternate between two languages.

The opposite of a 1P/1L setting is one where all the people that children meet up with alternate between the same two languages. This we can call the 1P/2L setting. In reality, it is unlikely that children will hear *all* the people around them actually speak two languages. Arno will be used to quite a few people speaking both German and French, though. He hears both his parents speak two languages, and anyone in the family on either side does too. But there will be some people, like the pediatrician or the baker at the corner shop, who speak just one language.

The setting where some of the people that children are very familiar with speak only one language to them, and others two (the 1P/1L & 1P/2L setting), as in the case of Ramon, is most likely the most common one.

In the following chapters I will be referring to the languages that the four main characters of this book are hearing mostly as Language A and Language Alpha, rather than as majority or minority language. The main language of each family's main residential community I've called Language A. The final box in this chapter indicates which of the two languages Lily, Arno, Ramon and Toshie are hearing that I will be calling Language A and Language Alpha in the following chapters. You may need this Language ID box for easy reference later on.

Language ID box	Which is Language A, and which is Language Alpha	
Child	*Language A*	*Language Alpha*
Lily	Dutch	Mandarin
Arno	French	German
Ramon	English	Spanish
Toshie	Japanese	Korean

Key points

- When children hear two languages from birth, they are growing up in a Bilingual First Language Acquisition (BFLA) setting. This setting involves newborn babies' caretakers speaking two different languages around the baby from the start. Typically, this situation occurs within the family, or the extended family.

- Children who have heard two languages from birth learn to understand two languages, Language A and Language Alpha. They may speak only one language, however, but of course there are many BFLA children who speak two.

- BFLA children all follow a particular pattern in learning to speak, regardless of whether they speak one or two languages. This goes from babbling over the production of single words to the combining of words into short sentences and later longer sentences that become more and more like the sentences adults would say. At first, BFLA children know just a few words, but soon they learn many more.

- The order in which BFLA children learn to say particular sorts of things (words and sentences) is fairly constant across children, regardless of the languages they are learning, but there are large differences between children in the ages at which they say them. These differences are the same in children growing up with just a single language. There is no evidence for the frequently heard claim that BFLA children as a group develop language more slowly than children growing up hearing just one language.

- BFLA children's two languages do not necessarily develop at the same rate. The extreme (but quite normal) case is the one where BFLA children speak only one language. BFLA children who speak only one language often take part in dilingual conversations in which one partner speaks Language A and the other one Language Alpha.

- Whether such dilingual conversations are possible at all will much depend on the adult conversation partners and whether they use monolingual rather than bilingual discourse strategies. The former support the use of only one language in a conversation, and the latter allow the use of two.

- From early on, BFLA children learn to speak the language that is expected of them. If no particular language is expected of them they tend to speak only one.

Activities and discussion points

1. Ask around in your circle of friends and family about whether they know anyone who was raised with two languages from birth. Try to get in touch with them and have a conversation with them about their early bilingual experience. What languages were involved? Did they learn to understand them? Did they learn to speak them? How do they feel about their early bilingualism?

2. Ask around in your circle of friends and family about whether they know anyone who is raising a child with two languages from birth. Try to get in touch with them and have a conversation with them about their child's overall linguistic development. What languages are involved? Does their child understand them both? Does their child speak them both?

3. Find people in your environment who because of their profession deal with young children (or find people who are studying in preparation of such professions). Possibilities are: pediatric nurses, pediatricians, family health practitioners, speech therapists, preschool teachers, childcare workers and the like. Have a conversation with two such individuals built around the following questions: would they advise people to raise their children with two languages? Why (not)? Be courteous with your interviewees even if you disagree with their points of view. Report on your findings in class and discuss the answers you gained in terms of some of the issues raised in this chapter.

Further reading

Sources introducing and defining BFLA

De Houwer (1990), Meisel (1989), Swain (1976)

On the family as the main setting for BFLA; on monolingual and bilingual discourse strategies

Lanza (1997, 2007)

On bilingual couples' changing relationship once children are born

Piller (2002)

Major steps in language development occur in the same order and at similar ages in BFLA and MFLA children despite large individual differences

De Houwer (2005), Patterson (1998), Pearson *et al.* (1993)

One in four bilingual families have children who speak just a single language

De Houwer (2007)

Rate of occurrence of 1P/1L, 1P/2L and 1P/1L & 1P/2L settings within bilingual families

De Houwer (2007), Yamamoto (2001)

2

From birth
to the
comprehension
of words

This chapter focuses on what BFLA children learn about language in the first year of life.

- First it gives a global view of important developmental processes in the first year of life.

- It then explains that BFLA children must learn the different sounds of their two languages.

- It also describes some aspects of the words that BFLA children hear.

- It then zooms in on the four BFLA children introduced in Chapter 1.

- It highlights different features of development for each child, so what is described for each child is necessarily selective.

- The descriptions taken together highlight:

  - the fact that BFLA children learn to distinguish between their two languages from early on;

  - how BFLA children start to try and articulate sounds themselves;

  - BFLA children's early comprehension of words;

  - the sensitivity that BFLA children may develop towards the languages spoken by the people around them.

Early interaction, socialization and maturation

Young children are, at first, not really able to communicate much. When they are born they are 'speechless', they are 'infants'. Gradually, babies learn to communicate with people they know. It is through these early interactions that babies become able to understand their world and the people in it.

This early learning through interaction with other people is the cornerstone of children's overall development and communicative functioning. Typically, these people are the baby's parents, grandparents, older siblings or hired childcare providers. Thus, infants tend to interact mostly with individuals who are several years older. Simply because of the difference in life experience, most of the people that young children interact with will have more skills and competence than they do, and will act as a guide and a model for them. The process through which children learn about human communication is called socialization.

Young children come to rely upon these important people in their lives, trust them and know them. Affective bonding with these people is very important, and children are eager to receive emotionally positive feedback from them. Young children are not simply 'passive consumers' of the attention they get: they bring their own developing minds and personalities to their interactions with the people familiar to them.

Children grow and change all the time. This process is called maturation. How much of the socialization around them children are able to interpret and act upon themselves very much depends on their level of maturation. There is a particular timetable or developmental path that all normally developing babies follow. For instance, as many young parents know all too well, it makes no sense to try and tell a three-month-old baby to stop crying. Very young babies are simply unable to understand what you say to them, and their crying appears to be something they cannot really control anyhow. And it makes no sense to teach nine-month-old babies to jump – at that age most cannot even walk.

Most parents know instinctively what their children will be able to do and 'take in' as they closely monitor their development and respond to the continuous changes in their children's abilities. There is also evidence that children's cognitive development partially depends on their socializing environments. Thus, children's development is the result of a complex interplay between their own developing neurological and physical abilities (their maturation) and the way their caretakers interact with them. Children's language learning is an integral part of their overall development and takes place at the intersection of interaction, socialization and maturation.

Infant detectives: Learning about sound

Just imagine that you are in a rain forest and you've never been in one before – you will be hearing all sorts of new and different sounds. At the beginning, you won't know what they mean, and each sound you hear may startle you and you may not know how to interpret it. But as you spend some more time in the rain forest, you'll soon start to recognize that some sounds are quite similar, and you'll have figured out they come from a spot of rain dropping on leaves, for instance, and are nothing to worry about. But once you have heard a very strong whooshing sound several times and have found yourself in a massive downpour each time you'll realize it's important to pay attention to different kinds of rain-sounds. You will have learned to put individual instances of different sounds into two major categories: the raindrop sound, which is harmless, and the downpour sound, which tells you you'd better find shelter.

Babies have to go through a similar process. They have to learn how the many different speech sounds they hear pattern into meaningful units. These units can be quite big, like the melody of a sentence. Sentence melodies (usually called **intonation patterns**) can signal different things, such as anger, a command, a statement or just where a sentence starts and stops. They differ from language to language, although there are overlaps between languages.

The units babies have to learn to recognize can also be quite small and operate at the level of speech sounds such as the 't' in 'take' or the 'o' in 'over'. These are called **phonemes**, and are also different for each language, although again, there are overlaps between languages.

BFLA infants have to learn to recognize different intonation patterns and phonemes in each of two languages.

Luckily for infants, languages have all kinds of cues that help infants to gradually detect which kinds of sounds it is important to pay attention to and what variations in sounds they can ignore without losing important information. The main reason why BFLA children have to learn to recognize these different intonation patterns and phonemes is that they help them to identify words in a sentence, i.e. where a word begins and ends. Identifying words is an important step towards learning to understand words. I explain a bit more about this in the next box.

Sound box   Why it is important that BFLA children learn to distinguish between the sounds of their two languages from early on

In some languages, one particular word can have different pitch variations or tones that each mean something different. For instance, Thai has five lexical tones. The same word (e.g. 'mai') can have meanings as different as those between 'wood' and 'not', depending on whether the word is said with a rising tone, a falling tone, in a steady high tone, in a steady mid tone or a steady low tone. In English the meanings of words do not change when you say them with a rising or falling tone. Instead, English relies on stress patterns. You can see how this works if you say the sentence 'did you put the vegetables in the fridge?'. You will notice that the final two syllables of 'vegetables' get very little stress indeed but the first one quite a bit, and that 'in' gets more stress than these two syllables – stress helps in defining the boundaries of English words.

In English (as in Thai) another cue that helps to identify where a wordt starts and stops is the order of phonemes. For instance, 'stick' is a fine word in English but 'tsick' is not – knowing that 'ts' cannot be at the beginning of a word in English helps you to know that 'gutsy' must be one word rather than two separate words 'gu' and 'tsy'. Word stress will also help you to figure this out.

Infants learning Thai will have to pay attention to variations in pitch at the word level. That will help in learning Thai.

But it won't help much if a BFLA child learning Thai and English tries to look for lexical tones in English. Suppose a Thai–English BFLA infant thinks that the word 'cow' said with falling intonation means 'horse', but that steady intonation signals 'cow'. And suppose that the infant is trying to find different meanings for all kinds of other English words pronounced with slightly different pitch patterns. This kind of strategy will get in the way of learning English. The cue that works for Thai doesn't work for English. In English, whether 'cow' is said with a rising, falling or steady pitch, it remains a cow.

On the other hand, a Thai–English BFLA child could, in theory, be approaching Thai on the basis of the sound rules for English words. The child could assume that the pitch or pitch variations for a word don't matter in Thai. A child with this assumption and learning strategy will fail to understand many words in Thai, since word pitch contours are important in order to distinguish between various meanings in Thai.

Clearly, BFLA Thai–English children need to discover the specific word-sounding cues for Thai, and the ones for English. Otherwise, they won't learn to identify Thai and English words, and to make sense of what people are saying. BFLA children learning other pairs of languages will have to learn to pay attention to other cues.

The words that BFLA children hear

By definition, BFLA children hear words in two languages. It is not enough that they learn to identify what the words are in each of their two languages. They must, of course, also learn to understand the words that people say to them, in whatever language they are. Otherwise, children will have trouble making sense of the world around them.

At the beginning, BFLA children's worlds are small. They typically live at home, and people talk to infants about food, drink, going to sleep, going for a walk, toys, the people in infants' environments and not a whole lot more.

Chances are that if people talk about these fairly basic things to a child in two languages, some of the words will be translations of each other (e.g. Spanish 'agua' and English 'water'). Such words are called **translation equivalents** or **TEs**.

A subgroup of translation equivalents that children hear consists of words that not only mean pretty much the same but that also sound pretty much the same, like German 'Bett' and English 'bed' (Schelletter, 2002). This set will be fairly large when children hear two languages that are closely related on the lexical level such as Danish and Swedish, or Spanish and Italian, and much smaller for historically much less related languages such as Mandarin and English. Words that mean and sound pretty much the same across languages are **cognates**.

Besides words from both their input languages that refer to the same thing BFLA children will also hear labels for things in one language only. There may be words that only mommy, or only daddy says. Mommy may never play with the toy truck, and so may not need to talk about it. And daddy may not be much involved with dressing the children, and so doesn't talk about their clothes with them. In a bilingual setting, this may lead to a kind of language specialization for some topics.

You don't get this language specialization in a monolingual situation, even though different speakers may talk about different things. For instance, if it is daddy who usually takes the kids to the zoo without mommy there, daddy will be the one naming the animals. If mommy doesn't really discuss animals, she will not be teaching children the words for them. But MFLA children will still know the words in their one language, even though they heard them from only one person.

In contrast, if the one person who talks to them about animals speaks French, and no one else talks to them about animals, children who hear French and German won't learn to understand or say any names for animals in German. Similarly, French–English two-year-old Caroline only said English 'cookie' and not French 'biscuit', simply because she had never heard the word French word for 'cookie' (Celce-Murcia, 1978).

In sum, the words that BFLA children hear are divided between two languages. Some of the words that young children hear in Language A will express things that they hear in Language Alpha as well. They may also hear some things discussed only in one language.

Furthermore, BFLA children might hear a lot of words in Language A but far fewer in Language Alpha. Alternatively, the input could be quite balanced in terms of the number of words that BFLA children hear in each language. Large differences in how many words BFLA children hear in each language will affect how many words they learn in each.

Lily: Lots of words

Lily's mother Xiu is sure that when she was eight months pregnant and her mother Mei came to visit from China, she felt Lily move in response to hearing Mandarin spoken for the first time (between Xiu and Mei). Indeed, unborn children can hear, and may be able to detect different languages before they are even born.

After Lily was born, grandma Mei stayed on for a while to help out so Lily heard quite a lot of Mandarin, both when Xiu or Mei talked to her and when mother and grandma spoke to each other. Father Hein spoke Dutch to Lily and to Xiu, but did not talk much to his mother-in-law because of his very limited speaking skills in Mandarin. However, his own mother, Rita, often visited the young family as well, and spoke Dutch to Lily and Xiu.

On the whole, Lily heard her mother speak mostly Mandarin. When she was four months old, she started to seem quite uneasy when she heard Xiu speak Dutch (for instance, when Hein came home from work). She would fidget and be unhappy. When Xiu switched back to Mandarin, Lily's unease was decidedly less and she even smiled!

For this different reaction to different languages to be possible, Lily must have heard a general difference between Mandarin and Dutch. And, indeed, young BFLA children who are not even six months old can distinguish between the two languages they have been hearing from birth. This ability is evident on a very general level only a few days after birth, but finer distinctions between separate phonemes can be made at four months of age.

Lily started to make little melodies when she was about eight months old. This was long after grandma Mei had left and Lily was basically taken care of by her mother, who spoke to her exclusively in Mandarin. Grandmother Rita took care of Lily one day a week, and on the weekends there was plenty of time to spend with daddy Hein. Rita and Hein addressed Lily only in Dutch. When Xiu heard her mother speak to anyone else, it was in Dutch as well.

The little melodies that Lily started to produce seemed to resemble little sentences, either in Mandarin or in Dutch. When she called out some unintelligible words with a Dutch-like intonation pattern, Hein would respond. When she sounded more Mandarin-like, it was Xiu who rushed to see what she wanted. This soon became a fairly clear pattern in the family. On weekends, Hein and Xiu usually knew exactly who Lily wanted to have attention from, depending on the intonation pattern she used.

On the whole, Lily was very vocal and responsive. She was usually in a good mood and very attentive to what the people around her did and said. This encouraged all people who met Lily to talk to her a lot. When she was one year old, Xiu estimated that Lily understood about 200 words in Mandarin. She checked this by filling out a form with a list of Mandarin words that young children are likely to understand. It was the pediatrician who asked her to do this. She happened to know that there was such a list in Mandarin that could be used by speech therapists to see whether children were developing slowly or quickly.

The pediatrician also asked Hein to fill out a similar list for Dutch. The result there was that Lily understood 120 words in Dutch. The fact that she understood more words in Mandarin than in Dutch reflects the fact that she spent far more time with a person who spoke Mandarin to her.

Lily's scores in Mandarin and Dutch separately were average to high compared to children learning only Mandarin or Dutch. And, of course, if you count up the number of words Lily understood in each of her languages (320), she was performing well above the level of monolingual children.

At age one, Lily was not saying real words, though, in spite of her rather large comprehension vocabulary. Indeed, at these early ages there is not necessarily a link between the number of words that BFLA infants understand and say.

Arno: Big babbler

Arno was born a little prematurely so he had to stay in the maternity hospital for a few weeks. In hospital, he didn't really hear much language at all; just a few French soothing words from his mother and the nurses, and a few German words from both his mother and his father.

When Arno finally was allowed to go home, things changed quite a bit! The whole family was there to meet him: both sets of grandparents, his uncle Peter from Germany with his three children, a French cousin and her husband and, of course, his parents. All day long there was a lot of talking going on in both French and German. The visitors stayed in the area for about 10 days (it happened to be a holiday break). Then, Arno and his parents went to Germany together with Peter and his children to enjoy the Bavarian countryside and the mountains. Even in Germany, Arno heard or overheard French and German every day.

Arno's early life continued to be quite busy socially. On a typical day, he would see three adults (including his parents) and a few older children. He would hear most of these people speak both French and German, though with variable levels of skill. They all understood both languages. Both Arno's parents worked from home, and they took turns in being 'on call' for Arno.

The speech Arno heard was mostly speech that he overheard, rather than that people talked directly to him individually. Although children can indeed learn from speech they overhear, the language used among adults and older children lacks the kind of specific exaggerated intonation patterns typical of speech addressed to infants. This kind of **infant-directed speech** or **IDS** helps direct infants' attention to specific sounds and words and plays an important role in children's language development.

Arno wasn't very vocal but people noticed how when he was five months old he started to look at their mouths very intently when they talked (even when they were not talking to him directly). This continued for several months. It seemed as if Arno was reading off what they were saying from their lips. Bruno got a bit worried, in fact, and thought Arno might be hard of hearing and that it was because of that that he paid so much attention to people's lips. But Arno's hearing was checked and turned out to be fine. What Bruno didn't know is that BFLA infants also use visual clues to help them to distinguish between languages, not only auditory ones. In fact, BFLA infants are able to distinguish between languages just based on differences between the lip movements that people make when they speak different languages.

When Arno was about seven months old, everybody noticed that he would look up and get excited if they talked about him and said his name. When his mother called him, he would look in her direction. But when she called out 'Marco!' he didn't pay much attention. Before age seven months he hadn't really paid any attention to his name. Alix and Bruno were pretty sure that now, at seven months, he recognized his name as something special.

At about eight months of age, Arno started to say things like 'bahbahbah' and 'googoogoo'. He would do this especially when he was alone in bed, prior to going to sleep. He seemed pretty happy when he was doing this and his parents decided not to disturb him while he was happily making these sounds. But they heard how he seemed to be testing out different sounds and repeating ever longer sequences. Arno never said these things when he was playing with people or sitting with people at the dinner table.

What Arno was doing there is called babbling. Most children babble at some point. Some, like Arno, babble for a long period of time (months), others much less. Babbling serves no clear communicative function, but can be seen as a kind of practicing. In babbling, children start to explore using their **articulatory organs** in some kind of controlled fashion. They explore what kind of sounds they can make with their lips and by opening and closing their mouths. These explorations involve their tongues, vocal cords and lungs as well.

When they heard Arno babbling, his parents weren't sure whether he was trying to mimic French or German. In fact, all they could hear that made them think of language at all was the fact that Arno was alternating between what sounded like consonants and vowels. Indeed, babbling typically involves infants producing several similar syllables right after each other. An upgrade in babbling occurs when infants produce different syllables in one breath, like 'bahgoo'.

Syllables exist in all languages and are the basic unit in which separate sounds or phonemes are put together. But just as Arno's parents couldn't really say whether the specific sounds in Arno's babbled syllables were French or German, scholars studying MFLA or BFLA aren't sure to what extent babbling already shows clear similarities with a particular language.

Ramon: Asking for words in two languages

Julia decided that she would have a home birth. Her husband, Alan, agreed. Ramon was born at home with both his parents there, his grandma Rosa and a midwife. All went well and right from the start Ramon heard his parents speak English to him. Grandma and the midwife greeted him in Spanish, and when the adults spoke to each other the midwife and Julia spoke either English or Spanish, but Rosa only Spanish and Alan only English.

Ramon was a very alert child who soon loved to smile and engage people in interaction. Julia took care of him most of the time, with or without Rosa there and then all the talk was in Spanish. When daddy Alan came home from work, Rosa usually was no longer there and all talk switched to English.

When Julia had to go back to work three months after giving birth, Ramon started going to a small day-care center where everyone spoke English. He went there three days a week. The other two workdays his grandma Rosa took care of him. She spoke to him in Spanish and took him with her to visit some of her Spanish-speaking friends.

The day-care providers were surprised to note how much Ramon already seemed to be saying at five months. They didn't understand a thing, of course, but he was a lot more vocal than the other children. And they were absolutely positive that at age eight months he had said 'hello'.

Also Rosa's friends commented on how 'talkative' Ramon was. And Rosa thought he might have said 'nana' for 'manzana' (Spanish for 'apple') when he was close to eight months old.

Nobody ever heard Ramon do much babbling, but just once, when he was nine months old, Julia heard him say 'boogahboogahdowdow'. At that time, he was already saying things that sounded like words, though.

At eight months Ramon had started pointing at all sorts of things as if to ask for their names. Everybody happily obliged, and said the names of things for him. What was really astonishing to Julia and Alan was that on weekends or evenings when they were both at home with Ramon (he was now close to 10 months old), he would point to something, look at Alan, and wait until Alan had said 'yes, that's a cup' (or whatever it was), and then he would look at Julia and point to the same object. When Julia then repeated what Alan had said Ramon would shake his head vehemently and point again and look at Julia very intently. He would only be happy when she told him what the thing was called in Spanish.

This way, Ramon learned to understand many words in English and their translations into Spanish. Not all BFLA children have Ramon's active interest in learning the names for things in each language, but by the time they are about one year old, BFLA children understand at least a few words that are translations of each other. Much will depend on what the people talk about in each of a BFLA child's language environment.

In Ramon's case, his environment both at grandma's and at home had very few toys in it, but all the more household objects, whereas the day-care center had lots of toys and relatively few household objects. At the day-care center, he learned lots of names for toys, but at home it was more things around the house that got talked about. Since his home was rather bilingual he learned about household objects in both languages (and if he didn't know a word in both languages, he would ask his parents!). Many names for toys he only knew in English, though.

Toshie: Highly sensitive to language choice

Atsuo and Yun were overjoyed when their daughter Toshie was born. Right from the start, Yun spoke Korean to Toshie but Japanese to everyone else, since nobody else in Toshie and Yun's environment spoke or even understood Korean. Yun's own parents were deceased and she had no Korean-speaking friends in Japan. For Yun it was a relief to be able to speak her home language again after so many years of just speaking Japanese. It felt very right to speak to Toshie in Korean.

Atsuo had never heard his wife speak Korean until the moment he heard her speak Korean to Toshie. Rationally, he thought it was only right that Yun should speak her own language to her child, but he felt somewhat disconnected when he heard Yun speak to Toshie in a language he did not understand. He shrugged it off and told himself that things would go better once the novelty of it all had worn off.

Toshie turned out to be a somewhat difficult child who was very picky about where she was willing to sleep and what she was willing to drink and eat. When she was five months old, she started to cry when Yun switched from speaking Korean to Toshie to speaking Japanese to Atsuo or his live-in parents. It's clear from this that Toshie was able to distinguish very well between Korean and Japanese, and that she had built up the expectation that her mother spoke only in one particular way: Korean.

Of course, it was impossible for Yun to communicate with Atsuo and her in-laws in anything but Japanese, but Toshie's crying did make things quite difficult. Yun tried to see how she could resolve the situation. She did not want to make language into a battleground, and started to try and speak some Japanese to Toshie when Atsuo or her in-laws were within earshot. At first, Toshie got very upset, but Yun persisted. Once Toshie was seven months old, she seemed to have become used to her mother speaking Japanese when other Japanese speakers were in the room, and Korean when they were alone.

Toshie started to move around quite early. She used a sort of sitting-and-sliding technique. The adults thought this was very cute and started asking Toshie to fetch all sorts of things for them. At age eight months, Toshie understood requests for fetching lots of different things. When she was a bit older, Toshie also loved to play social games like peek-a-boo, and she was very good at pointing at her nose, ears, mouth and head when so asked. She was able to do all this both with Korean and Japanese words.

If Yun inadvertently said a Korean word to Toshie when Japanese speakers were present, Toshie stopped in her tracks, looked at her mother with a quizzical look on her face, and giggled in a sort of embarrassed way. Yun was then quick to correct herself and repeat the word in Japanese, and Toshie seemed pleased with that. Toshie's reaction to Yun saying a Japanese word to her when they were alone was much more strong, though: Toshie would burst into tears if this happened, and it took Yun a lot of time to try and calm her down. Yun tried to avoid saying anything in Japanese when she was alone with Toshie.

Toshie loved hearing children's songs. Yun had some Korean songs as well as some in Japanese. She put on the Korean ones only when no speakers of Japanese were present. The Japanese songs were reserved for the times that there were. Also, Toshie would have it no other way.

One day, Yun and Toshie were out shopping. On the street, Yun heard two Korean tourists discussing with each other where to find a famous department store. Yun heard that they were about to go in the wrong direction, so she took the initiative to talk to the two tourists in Korean and explain where they should go. Toshie observed this brief conversation with obvious amazement, and when the tourists went on their way she turned around to stare at them until they were out of view. Toshie was very quiet afterwards. She was apparently quite stunned by this linguistically unusual encounter and needed to sort it out in her mind.

Key points: Bilingual language development in the first year of life

- By the time of their first birthdays, Lily, Arno, Ramon and Toshie were all able to understand words and phrases from each of their two input languages. Indeed, by the time they are one year old, BFLA children have learned enough about the sounds of their two languages to be able to understand words and phrases in each.

- Learning about the separate sounds of each language takes some time, and starts off with distinguishing between the two languages on a more global level earlier. Lily and Toshie showed clear signs of distinguishing between their two languages between four and five months. But, of course, the earlier lack of such signs doesn't imply they could not hear the difference between Language A and Language Alpha before. In fact, newborn babies can already distinguish between a language they have heard in the womb and another language.

- Lily, Arno, Ramon and Toshie started showing signs of understanding words and phrases at different ages. They also differed in the number of words they understood in each language, and in the total number of words they understood across both languages. Furthermore, Arno and Ramon understood about equal numbers of words in each of their languages, whereas Lily and Toshie understood more words in the language they heard spoken to them most frequently (Mandarin and Japanese, respectively). Indeed, there are large differences between BFLA children in how many words they understand at a given age. In addition, there may be large differences between a BFLA child's two languages as far as the number of words understood in each is concerned.

- Some of the four children reacted strongly to their parents' choice of language. Others did not. In response to this, some parents changed or persevered in their patterns of language choice. This shows the complex interplay between children's own developing personalities and the people who constitute their language-learning environment. Patterns of interaction concerning language choice, then, are already formed before BFLA children can speak.

- None of our four children really talked much before they were one year old. However, they had all started babbling at some point, but differed in the exact ages at which they started babbling, for how many months they continued to babble, and how often they babbled. Whatever babbling practice they had had made them ready for starting to say things that sounded like words. But that's for the next chapter!

Activities and discussion points

1. Visit the website of the Vancouver infant studies lab under the direction of Dr Janet Werker and, in particular, the part of it on visual language discrimination in infancy at http://www.psych.ubc.ca/~jwlabmgr/SiteNew/Pictures.html. Look at the various pictures and movies. In particular, watch the examples of silent French and English stimuli. Can you spot the difference?

2. Visit the website http://www.vocaldevelopment.com/. Click on the button 'Learn about and listen to vocalizations from different developmental levels'. Then go to the button 'Basic Canonical Syllables' and listen to all the examples. Do these sounds sound like language to you? Why (not)? (This website was developed by Dr Ertmer at Purdue University in the United States.) Have a class discussion about this.

3. Find a family with a child under the age of one who is hearing two languages at home. Have a conversation with the parents about the child's language development. Focus on these three questions: (a) do the parents think their child can hear the difference between the two languages? Why (not)?; (b) does the child say anything or make any sounds that make the parents think of language? If so, ask parents to elaborate; (c) does the child understand his or her name, or anything else?

Evaluate the answers you got in function of the child's age and what you learned in this chapter. If several of your classmates also do this activity, but with different families, have a group discussion comparing your results to each other and to the key points of this chapter.

Further reading

Books with a lot of information on BFLA children's language development in the first year of life

Cruz-Ferreira (2006), De Houwer (2009, the first halves of Chapters 5 and 6), Leopold (1970), Ronjat (1913)

Newborn infants can distinguish between the language their mothers spoke during pregnancy and other languages

Moon & Fifer (2000)

Cognitive development partially depends on children's socializing environments

Bornstein (2002), Bornstein *et al.* (1996, 1998), Hart & Risley (1995)

BFLA infants' early speech perception and comprehension

Bosch & Sebastián-Gallés (2001), Werker & Byers-Heinlein (2008)

A study of infant-directed speech involving a BFLA child

Van de Weijer (1997)

Understanding words in two languages

De Houwer *et al.* (2006)

Bilingual babbling

De Houwer (2009, Chapter 5), Poulin-Dubois & Goodz (2001)

On the link between early word comprehension and production in BFLA

De Houwer (2009, Chapter 6)

Large differences in how much children hear of each language affects the number of words they know in each

Pearson *et al.* (1997)

3

Saying words and starting to combine them

This chapter continues where the last one left off and focuses on BFLA children's early speech production, which typically takes off in the second year of life:

- It discusses BFLA children's use of speech sounds.

- It explains how BFLA children start to try and say words.

- It discusses how BFLA children learn to say more and more words.

- It talks about BFLA children's use of translation equivalents.

- It says a bit about BFLA children's first word combinations.

- ...And shows how BFLA children can often already choose the socially appropriate language when needed.

Right from the start, the chapter zooms in on the four BFLA children you got to know in Chapters 1 and 2. As in Chapter 2, this chapter highlights different features of development for each child, so what is described for each child is necessarily selective.

Before you continue, it may be a good idea to reread the sections on each of the four children in Chapter 2.

Lily: Changing places

By age one, Lily understood a lot of words both in Mandarin and in Dutch. She would also say what sounded like little Mandarin or Dutch sentences, but these were completely incomprehensible. One weekend, though, Lily very clearly said 'pakke!', with stress on the first syllable and no stress on the second. For a moment, her parents Hein and Xiu didn't know what was going on – but then Xiu said to Hein (in Dutch) 'She means she wants to get that cookie!'. And yes, Lily said 'pakke' while pointing to a cookie lying on a kitchen counter, and in a tone of voice somewhere between a question and a command. 'Pakke' is a Dutch infinitive meaning 'get' or 'pick up' (for speakers of Dutch – I write it here without a final 'n' to show how it is normally pronounced).

Lily's use of 'pakke' is a typical example of young children using holophrases. These are single words that are apparently used with the meaning of a full sentence, as in this case: 'there's a cookie and I want you to get it for me so I can eat it' – you might think this is an overinterpretation, but that's what it's all about: children's holophrases are *interpreted* as meaning something. Whether Lily really meant that she wanted her parents to get her the cookie is not certain, but Hein agreed with Xiu that that was the most likely explanation, given the context in which she said 'pakke'. Like other parents, Hein and Xiu were very eager to try and figure out what it was that Lily was trying to say.

In fact, parents are quite excited when their children say their first words. Hein and Xiu were no exception, and Hein quickly called his mother Rita on the phone to tell her that Lily had just said her first 'real' word, and that it was in Dutch! Xiu was, of course, also excited, but when she tried to get Lily to say 'get' in Mandarin, she had no luck. Still, she emailed her mother in China straightaway to tell her the big news, and also to make some more arrangements for her upcoming trip to China.

Xiu and Lily left a week later to spend time with the family in China for seven weeks. Hein might be able to make a quick visit in that period if he could fit it into his Asian business trip.

In China, Lily naturally received a lot of attention from all the family members who had not ever seen her, and from her grandmother Mei, who had only seen her for two months right after she was born. Everyone was delighted that Lily was able to understand many simple requests in Mandarin. Grandma Mei loved playing the game 'where is your nose?' (or ears, or eyes, or other body part) with her, where she asked Lily a question and Lily pointed to the right body part.

In the first two weeks, Lily didn't say much. Of course, she had only said one word before, but she had also said longer stretches of sounds with a Dutch or Mandarin intonation pattern. None of that now. Lily was very interested in all the people she met, though, and eager to please them by laughing a lot, smiling at them, fetching things for them and so forth. But she did not say anything that sounded like language. It was as if she had to get used to the fact that everything was now in Mandarin, and that so many people spoke the language she had earlier only heard her mother speak.

Then, after two weeks, Lily said three different Mandarin words on one day! It was grandma Mei who was there to hear them. When Xiu came home, she was so sorry she missed hearing these! But no problem – the next few days, Lily said these words quite a few times more on different occasions, so Xiu had plenty of opportunity to hear them. Lily used her three Mandarin words with seemingly holophrastic meanings.

Lily's box Her first three Mandarin words		
Mandarin word (in Pinyin)	English translation	Context of use
ma1ma5	mommy	when Lily wanted something to eat or drink
bu4	no	when Lily didn't want to eat, drink or do something that someone else was trying to have her eat, drink or do
kai1 (men2)	open the door	when Lily wanted to get out of her crib, or go and see someone in another room (and the door was closed), or when she wanted to have her clothes taken off to take a bath

Except for 'no' and 'open the door' to go and see someone in another room (when the door was closed), Lily's meanings were fairly different from the adult meanings of 'mommy' and 'open the door'. Indeed, children have to find the right matches between particular word forms and the meanings these forms are used within adult speech. At first, children's matches are quite changeable. Gradually, they become more like those of adults.

After a few days of just sticking to three Mandarin words, Lily started to say other words as well. After a month in China, when she was close to 14 months old, she had learned to say a total of 12 Mandarin words but no longer said any Dutch words.

Then daddy Hein came to visit! Xiu repeatedly talked to Lily about him coming in the days before he would get there, and Lily was very excited. However, when he arrived, she felt shy and seemed not to understand what he said to her in Dutch. Hein didn't pay much attention to that. He was just so happy to be reunited with his family again. But in the five days he had time to spend with Lily and Xiu, Lily continued not to understand anything Hein said to her. Lily also watched with curious attentiveness when Xiu talked to Hein in Dutch. Hein was a bit disappointed, but there was nothing he could do for now.

After Hein left, Lily continued to add more Mandarin words to her spoken repertoire. When she was nearly 15 months old, it was time to go back to the Netherlands. Of course, the family in China was unhappy to see Xiu and Lily leave, but they agreed to have video conversations via the internet. And next year there would be another visit.

Back in the Netherlands, Lily at first didn't understand any Dutch. But soon after she started spending one day a week with grandma Rita again. Much to Hein's relief, she relearned to understand many of the words she had forgotten. And when she was 16 months old, she started saying a few Dutch words too.

For a few months, Lily continued saying Mandarin words to Xiu. When she said Dutch words, Hein or Rita were present. Xiu might be there, too. But when Hein was together with Xiu, and Lily said a word in Mandarin, it was always Xiu who responded rather than Hein, although he did understand the Mandarin words his daughter said. This pattern reminded them of a year earlier, when Lily would say unintelligible 'sentences' with a Dutch or Mandarin intonation pattern, and Hein would respond to the former, and Xiu to the latter.

When Lily was 19 months old, Xiu got a job for four days a week. Luckily, grandma Rita was happy to take care of Lily while Xiu and Hein were at work. For Lily this meant that she now heard Dutch most of the time rather than Mandarin. Two months later, Lily was saying her first word combination: 'oma kijke!' (Dutch for 'look, grandma!').

Arno: Picking up speed

Arno's earlier babbling made way for words when he was 13 months old. In a single day, he said his first German and his first French word. They were 'ape' (an attempt at German 'Apfel', apple) and 'mimou' (an attempt at French 'Minou', the cat's name). The meaningless babbling he had been practicing before now gave way to endless pre-sleep monologues alternating between 'ape' and 'mimou', which sometimes came out correctly as 'minou'. Unlike Lily, Arno didn't seem to mean anything else with these first words except giving something a name. He said each while simply pointing to an apple and the cat, respectively. He took no further interest in either, and his tone of voice each time was quite matter-of-fact, and not questioning or demanding.

Earlier, Arno had been pointing to a lot of pictures and objects saying 'huh?'. This was accompanied by a very exaggerated questioning expression on his face. He then expected any older person in the room to say what was on the picture or what the object was called. After he started saying words himself, Arno continued to ask for the names of pictures and objects, but now he would accompany his query with 'ka?', possibly an imitation of French 'quoi?' (what), and his querying expression would be much less exaggerated than before. You could call this 'ka?' a kind of holophrase, because it meant a whole complex idea like 'there is something I've noticed and I want to know what it's called and I'm asking you to tell me'.

Arno started using a new tactic though. After having asked for and received a name for an object, he would look at the person saying it with a renewed questioning expression, and would say 'ka? ka?'. If the person then repeated the word in the same language, Arno would vehemently shake his head and repeat his request. Alix, Arno's mother, figured out that perhaps Arno was asking for the name in the other language! She tried it, and it worked. Soon all the people who Arno asked a word from got used to saying it to him twice: once in French, and once in German.

It would go like this: Arno once pointed to a picture of a sailing boat. He asked his father Bruno: 'ka?'. Bruno then said: 'Das ist ein *Schiff*. Ich meine, auf *deutsch* ist das ein *Schiff*. Aber auf *französisch* heißt das *bateau*. *Bateau*. Also, *Schiff*, und *bateau*.' ('That's a boat. I mean, in German that's a boat. But in French that's called a boat. So, boat, and boat' – but of course the words for 'boat' here are different in German and French). You'll notice that Bruno here is actually naming the different languages. Whether Arno understood those names before he was two isn't certain. But because everyone in Arno's family was speaking two languages to him it wasn't possible to use the strategy that parents in a 1P/1L setting often use, namely, to refer to 'the language that mommy speaks', or 'daddy's language' in order to make things more concrete for young children and to avoid having to use the rather abstract names for languages.

By the time he was 15 months old, Arno said many different words in both French and German. He addressed everyone he knew in both languages, except people he would meet in shops and who talked to him only in French. He would respond to them using only French words.

The words Arno said sounded like either French or German words, but they often sounded quite different from the adult versions. Arno would leave out some sounds (see the light gray part in Arno's box), or he would replace sounds with others (see the darker gray part in the box).

Arno's box	The sounds of words		
Arno's word	*The adult version*	*English translation*	*What Arno did with the sounds*
pielen	spielen (German)	play	left off the initial 's'
bane	cabane (French)	little house or hut	left off the initial 'ca-'
Kudetier	Kuscheltier (German)	cuddly toy	pronounced 'sh' ('sch') as 'd'
éfesant	éléphant (French)	elephant	pronounced 'l' as 'f', a sharp 'é' as 'e' in 'the', and pronounced 'f' ('ph') as a soft 's'

Both BFLA and MFLA children often make mistakes in pronouncing words when they start to talk. Deleting or substituting sounds are the result of using what is called **phonological processes**. Because of their use of phonological processes, children may be very hard to understand.

Arno also said some words that sounded entirely adult-like or close, like 'tatine' (French 'tartine', sandwich) or 'noch!' (German for 'more'). But when it wasn't quite clear what word Arno was trying to say, the adults around him usually did have a good idea of which language he was aiming at because of the overall shape of the word. They interpreted words with two syllables where Arno had placed the stress on the first syllable as being German, and asked him in German what he meant (an example is Arno's '*Katte*' for German '*Katze*', cat). But when they heard Arno say a word with two syllables where the stress was on the final syllable, they asked him in French what he meant (an example here is 'be*ron*' for French 'bibe*ron*', bottle). In German, words tend to have their main stress on the first syllable, whereas French has many more instances where word stress is at the end of a word.

Some of Arno's words weren't clearly German or French but worked in either, like 'gijaf', which could be an attempt at German 'Giraf' or French 'giraffe' (both with stress on the second syllable), but with the r's replaced by /j/ (the first sound of 'you').

Between age 15 and 16 months, Arno learned to say many new words in each language. When people asked Alix which language he spoke best, she couldn't say. She thought he knew just about the same number of words in German as in French. She found out about word lists in French and German that speech therapists used to see whether children were developing on track, and just for fun she filled out both lists. It turns out that Arno said many of the words on each list and must have a total production vocabulary of around 700 words.

At age 16 months, Arno started combining words into short sentences. He would say things like 'mama beiben' (German for 'Mama bleiben'; mommy stay) or 'faire dodo' (French meaning go to sleep). Once in a while, he would say a two-word combination consisting of a French and a German word, like 'pompier schnell!' when he was playing with his fire truck and little firemen. He put the French word 'pompier' (fireman) together with the German word 'schnell' (fast). But usually his two-word combinations were entirely in German, or entirely in French.

Ramon: Saying words in two languages

At age nine months, Ramon was heard to say things that sounded like words to the people around him, but they weren't sure. When he was 10 months old, though, Ramon clearly said 'awa!' as he reached for his bottle of water. That was a rendition of Spanish 'agua' (water), or at least, that's how Julia, his mother, interpreted Ramon's 'awa'. A few days later, the day-care providers reported that Ramon had said 'no!' when another child had wanted to take his banana away. This is a word that works both in English and in Spanish.

Between 10 and 12 months, Ramon added some more words to his repertoire. He no longer said 'awa', though, because he was now more interested in drinking juice. That he called 'u-o', pronouncing just the vowels of Spanish 'jugo' (juice; as for 'awa', you see here Ramon's use of a phonological process). About two-thirds of his nearly 20 words by age one were in English, though (for instance, he said 'tuck' for 'truck').

By age 15 months, Ramon had added another 20 words or so to his production repertoire. The people who knew him could understand him fairly well, but when grandma Rosa took Ramon to visit her friends, they weren't sure what he was wanting to say, and Rosa had to explain. It is quite normal that children under the age of two are not easily comprehensible to unfamiliar people.

Whereas he apparently didn't say any purely Spanish words at the day care (or, at least, the day-care workers hadn't noticed any, even though they understood a bit of Spanish), Ramon used both Spanish and English words at home. There wasn't much of a pattern there though. Ramon would say either Spanish or English words to each of his parents. And since both his parents understood Spanish (daddy Alan didn't understand a lot, but had no problem with the simple words his one-year-old said), Ramon didn't have to worry about getting what he wanted and needing the 'right' language for it. At his grandma Rosa's, Ramon did tend to use mostly Spanish words, but occasionally he said an English one too.

For some words, though, even the people who knew him had trouble understanding what he was aiming at. They sometimes found it hard to decide which language he was using. At the day-care center, the adults just assumed that Ramon was talking English, but perhaps when they didn't understand what he was saying he was actually attempting to say a Spanish word. Likewise, when he was with grandma, some of the words he was saying that she couldn't figure out might have been attempts at English, who knows. She didn't know enough English to find out.

At home, Julia and Alan didn't have any assumptions about which language Ramon was attempting, and if they didn't understand him they tried to think of words in either language that he might be trying to say. On the whole, Julia and Alan understood Ramon much better than Rosa or the day-care providers.

Although Ramon understood many words for the same thing in both languages (translation equivalents; see Chapter 2), the words he *said* didn't contain any translation equivalents in the beginning. So when he was leaving he would say 'bye bye' and not 'adios', and when he wanted his mother he would say 'mamá' and not 'mommy'. Yet, Ramon continued to be interested in hearing the names for things in both languages, as he had when he was younger.

The fact that Ramon understood many translation equivalents but didn't say any yet shows that early language comprehension is one thing, and early language production quite another. Another phenomenon that demonstrates the difference between comprehension and production is that children understand many more words than they say.

Between age 15 and 17 months, Ramon added just a few words to his production vocabulary. Then, when he was 17 months old, Ramon all of a sudden rapidly learned to say many more new words in each language. After about a month's time, he was saying over 200 new words. This explosion in word production is commonly called the vocabulary spurt. Not all children experience such a sudden and dramatic increase in the number of different words they say, but many do (like Arno earlier).

In BFLA children, the vocabulary spurt may not be equally strong in each language. Although Ramon learned many new words in each of his two languages at the same age, he did learn to say many more new words in English than in Spanish. Remember that when he first started to talk, he already said more words in English. This most likely reflects the fact that he spent somewhat more time with people who spoke English to him than with people who talked to him in Spanish. When he was 16.5 months old, his grandma Rosa had left on a long trip to Mexico. This meant that Ramon was spending even more time at the English-speaking day-care center and heard less Spanish. His relatively greater increase in the number of English words reflects the fact that he heard a lot more English than Spanish.

At the same time that he experienced a vocabulary spurt, Ramon's production vocabulary now contained several translation equivalents. For instance, when he wanted something from his father, he would sweetly call out 'daddy?' but he also ran to the door saying 'papi! papi!' (daddy! daddy!) in Spanish when he heard his father come home from work.

Ramon's box	Translation equivalents	
Ramon's Spanish word	*Ramon's English word*	*Context*
aga (for 'agua')	wate (for 'water')	when he wanted a drink of water
adios!	bye bye	when he was leaving
aqui!	here!	when he wanted the dog to come to him

Whether the Spanish and English versions of Ramon's translation equivalents meant exactly the same thing isn't certain. Sometimes they clearly did, such as when he waved goodbye to Julia saying 'adios! bye bye!'. At other times, you might suspect they didn't. For instance, Ramon called the family car 'auto' (or something sounding like it), but when he saw other cars on the street that he especially liked he would point and say 'car'. He never called the family car 'car', and he never called other cars 'auto'. Ramon used both words in a more restricted meaning than they have in adult speech. This is an example of **underextension**.

In contrast, Ramon sometimes also used **overextension**. That's when he used a word with a wider meaning than in adult speech. For instance, he called any hot drink 'café' (Spanish for 'coffee') or 'coffee'. He tended to use 'coffee' at the day care, and 'café' at home (actually, when he asked for 'café' or 'coffee' he got cooled down hot chocolate). The origin of Ramon's overextension here probably lies in the fact that Julia and Alan used to say to Ramon: 'come, let's drink coffee together!', when they wanted him to come and sit at the table while they were having coffee and Julia gave Ramon a cup just like hers, first with juice in it, and later with a chocolate drink after Julia would ask Ramon: ¿quieres un café? (would you like some coffee?).

Ramon continued to learn many new words. When he knew a total of about 400 words, he said his first word combination (he was around 20 months of age): 'no daddy!', when his father wanted to scoop him up and get him ready for bed, and right after that: 'wanna pay!' ('pay' instead of 'play'; young children often have trouble saying two consonants right after the other). Even though grandma Rosa had come back from her trip and Ramon heard much more Spanish again, a two-word combination in Spanish appeared only two months later: 'mamá aquí!' (Spanish for 'mommy here!'), said to his mother when he wanted her to sit with him and read him a book.

Toshie: A slow start

Toshie was saying a few things when she was one year old. However, what she said was incomprehensible to her family. Yet, Toshie appeared to be saying things in specific contexts that might be meaningful to her. She said a long 'shhhh' when she heard water running out of the kitchen tap. A few days later, she said a long 'shhhh' when she heard her mother take a shower. Yet later she said a long 'shhhh' when she was walking past a canal with her grandma. It wasn't clear whether Toshie meant anything specific or was trying to name the water or water sounds. She would also emit a sound like 'woo' when she was throwing little balls at her father, and she would say 'woo' also when she saw a bird fly.

Toshie said about six or seven such sounds that were pretty much the same in form for many weeks, and she would say one particular sound in contexts that were somewhat similar. Exactly what she meant wasn't clear though. These kinds of sounds are called **phonetically consistent forms**. They are not words in any real sense. Like some other children, Toshie used these phonetically consistent forms for a long time. In fact, her parents were starting to worry that she was so late in saying her first real word.

Just when they had decided to take Toshie to the pediatrician to see if everything was OK, Toshie said her first real word: 'taiyo!' (Japanese for 'sun'). She said this when she switched on the main light in her bedroom and pointed to the lamp. Yun, who had just stepped into the room with her, was overjoyed to hear Toshie say a real word. She hugged and kissed Toshie and repeated in Japanese: 'taiyo! taiyo!'. Toshie was 17 months old.

Toshie's first word was gradually followed by some others. Most of them sounded like Japanese words, and a few were in Korean. Toshie would sometimes say a Korean word to her grandparents but they would not understand and ask her what she meant. After a while, Toshie stopped saying Korean words to anyone except her mother. She said Japanese words to anybody, though, including her mother. Yun continued to speak Korean to Toshie when she was alone with her, and Japanese when others were present. Toshie did not seem to make any distinction between these contexts herself yet. That is, she did not limit her own Korean words to when she was alone with Yun, and she said Japanese words to her mother also when no other people were present.

When Toshie said a word, she did so very precisely. She articulated very carefully, and sounded surprisingly adult in the relatively few words she knew. When she was 19 months old, Toshie started to say many more words. Again, these were said with great precision.

However, the many new words that Toshie said were all in Japanese. She continued to say the few Korean words she had said earlier, but after a while, Korean words disappeared from

Toshie's speech entirely. By the time Toshie was 21 months old, she was just saying Japanese words. Her mother wasn't worried about this. On the contrary, she was happy that Toshie was learning to speak.

And Yun was overjoyed when at age 22 months Toshie said her first two-word combination: 'Toshie shu-u!' (Japanese for 'Toshie do'). Toshie said this when she wanted to tie her shoelaces herself rather than let her mother help her. Toshie continued to learn to say many new words after she had said her first little sentence, but they were all in Japanese. Also, the later two-word combinations she said drew on her Japanese vocabulary, and were exclusively in Japanese. Yun didn't worry and thought she would teach Toshie to say sentences in Korean later on. Yun continued to speak Korean to Toshie, and Toshie would respond in Japanese, showing that she understood her mother's Korean perfectly well. Here, we see examples of dilingual conversations (see Chapter 1).

Toshie's two-word combinations were hard to describe from a grammatical point of view. They did have fairly clear functions, though, and hearing Toshie say two-word combinations certainly helped her family to better understand her. Through using two-word combinations, Toshie was able to express much more than she had before, and she now seemed to really enjoy talking. She continued to articulate fairly clearly, and it was rare that she said a word her family members could not understand. Yet people who didn't know her still did have some trouble understanding her at first.

Toshie's box Examples of two-word combinations

describing what somebody was doing

'grandmother fish' (context: grandmother was drawing a fish)

expressing what belonged to whom

'bag daddy' (context: looking underneath a low table and finding her father's briefcase)

describing some characteristic of a particular entity

'dolly pretty' (context: Yun had just combed the hair of Toshie's favorite doll)

requesting something

'mommy sit' (context: Toshie wanted her mother to sit down so she could read a book for Toshie)

refusing something

'no carrot' (context: Toshie was having dinner but pushed away her bowl with parboiled carrots)

All utterances are shown in their English translation, but Toshie said them in Japanese

Key points: *From first words to word combinations*

- As for MFLA children, the second year of life brings great changes in BFLA children's linguistic skills: they actually start to talk! Some children start 'talking' by saying what appears to be little sentences with melodies (Lily) , or they say much shorter stretches of sounds that seem to have some meaning for children (Toshie). Others prepare themselves by babbling a lot (Arno), and yet others dive right in (Ramon) – right into the production of what the adults around them interpret as being real words.

- At first, like MFLA children, BFLA children say just one word at the time. These words have some kind of global meaning (holophrases), and children's meanings may differ quite a bit from the adult meanings (Lily's 'open the door'). Also, the forms of children's words are often quite distinct from the adult forms (phonological processes). This makes many young children hard to understand, regardless of whether they are monolingual or bilingual.

- As BFLA children continue to learn to say more words, they continue to learn to understand more words in both languages (Arno). They will also say words in two languages, although this may not last, and BFLA children may stop saying words in one of their languages (Toshie). If BFLA children do say words in both languages, some of these may be translation equivalents (Arno, Ramon; Lily also used these).

- If young BFLA children are in a place where they hear everyone speak just one language and they have not really heard these people talk another language, they usually will say words from just that same language (Lily, Arno, Ramon, Toshie). If they are with people who have mostly spoken two languages to them they will also feel free to use words from either language (Arno, Ramon, Toshie). BFLA children who have usually been addressed in Language A by a person they know to speak Language Alpha too will very often stick to just Language A with that person, regardless of who else is present (Lily).

- At some point in the second year of life, but certainly by age two, BFLA children start to combine words with each other into little two-word 'sentences'. These express relations between objects, people, actions, events or qualities, but usually show little grammatical structure. As such, they are not yet real sentences. This development mirrors that in MFLA children.

- There is a great deal of variation between BFLA children and between their languages in the ages at which the major language developments in the second year take place. I show this in the next box.

Variation box Different timings for major developments in the second year			
What?	Child	Language A	Language Alpha
first word	Lily	12 months	13 months
	Arno	13 months	13 months
	Ramon	10 months	10 months
	Toshie	17 months	18 months
saying 200 different words	Lily	18 months	22 months
	Arno	15 months	15 months
	Ramon	18 months	20 months
	Toshie	19 months	n.a.
the first two-word combination	Lily	21 months	23 months
	Arno	16 months	16 months
	Ramon	20 months	22 months
	Toshie	22 months	n.a.
started saying words from each language for the same thing (translation equivalents)	Lily	15 months	
	Arno	14 months	
	Ramon	16 months	
	Toshie	n.a.	

n.a. = not applicable

- The box you see here summarizes some points about Lily, Arno, Ramon and Toshie that I made earlier in this chapter, but also adds some developments I haven't discussed before. The box shows differences between the children in the ages at which they said their first word, said 200 words in one of their languages, said their first two-word combination and their first translation equivalent. My choice of 200 words here is a bit arbitrary, but when children have 200 words in their production repertoire they usually know a variety of different kinds of words that allow them to speak about a wide variety of things. Usually when children have 200 words in a language they do not yet put words together though.

- For the first word, there is a difference of seven months between Ramon and Toshie. That is a large difference in a period of 17 months. There is a difference of six months between Arno and Toshie in the age at which they said their first two-word combination. The differences in the ages at which the children first said 200 words in one of their languages are not that great, however. Neither are the differences between the ages for the first production of translation equivalents.

- You see here that the child who was the youngest when he said 200 words in a language was also the fastest to start saying two-word combinations (Arno). The child who was the last to reach the 200 word mark was also the last to start combining words (Toshie). Indeed, for many children there is a relation between the number of words they say and their use of combinatorial language (that is, word combinations).

- The variation we see for BFLA children is very similar to the variation there is among MFLA children. For BFLA children there is the added variation between their two languages. Their two languages may develop at a similar pace (Arno), or there may be smaller or larger differences between their two languages (Lily, Ramon). The variation may be so great that BFLA children develop speaking skills just in one language (Toshie). They may also temporarily lose a language and then relearn it (Lily) .

- Much of the variation between one BFLA child's two languages can be explained by differences in the relative frequency with which children hear each of their languages (Lily, Ramon). A language that is heard more often will stand a good chance of being better known. Children who hear each of their languages about equally often will have a more equal skill in each (Arno). The absence of socialization patterns that encourage children to use one of their input languages may have a direct effect on how often or even whether they use it themselves (Toshie).

- The variation between different BFLA children in how fast they develop their 'best' language may also, to a large extent, be due to input factors. Future research will have to explore this further.

Activities and discussion points

1. If you speak two languages (also if you don't speak them equally well): Are there any topics you can talk about very easily in one language but not the other? Select 10 topics that you can talk about in at least one language. Draw up a little table in which you check off for each language which topic you can discuss easily. Have a conversation about this with other students in your class and compare notes. Why do you think there are these differences between topics in how easily you can discuss them in one language versus the other?

2. Do this activity with a friend who can help out with the filming. Find a family with a BFLA child who is nearly two years old and who is learning two languages you understand (it's enough that you yourself speak just one of them). Ask whether you can come and visit at a time when the family is not having dinner and the child is awake and alert. Ask whether you can make a video recording of you playing with the child for half an hour using the child's own toys, and say that you'll bring a friend to do the recording. It's fine if the parents are in the room during the recording. Explain that you are studying child language development.

Once you get the OK, make your video recording (but give the child a few minutes to get acquainted with you and the filmer first). I suggest you bring an attractive children's book without words that you can use during the session to elicit speech from the child. You can then give this book to the child afterwards as a gift. Play with the child but try to elicit as much speech from him/her as you can. This may be a difficult task in itself.

While you play with the child, record what is going on. When you get back home, analyze all or part of the following (you can do this activity with a friend in your class, but it is best to do this as soon as possible after the recording):

(a) which words or phrases did the child appear to understand?

(b) could you mostly understand the child (you might have needed some time to 'warm up')?

(c) if you could, what were the child's words and what do you think they meant?

(d) did you notice any 'strange' uses of words? Explain.

(e) was the child saying only single words or already seeming to combine words?

3. Re-read all the information about Toshie in Chapters 1, 2 and 3. What do you think of Toshie's lack of Korean words by the time she is saying her first two-word combination? Do you think things could have gone differently? If so, how? Have a class discussion about this.

Further reading

Word lists: the CDI

In discussing Lily (Chapter 2) and Arno (this chapter), I mentioned lists of words that speech therapists can use to see if young children know the number of words expected for their age. These lists are adaptations of the MacArthur Communicative Development Inventory (CDI). This is a list of words that young children commonly understand and say where parents or other people who know a child very well have to check off which words the child understands or says. It was first developed for English (Fenson *et al.*, 1993), but since has been adapted to many other languages, including Mandarin, Malay, Yiddish and Spanish. You can find more information about the CDI through the official CDI website at http://www.sci.sdsu.edu/cdi/.

Books with a lot of information on BFLA children's language development in the second year of life

Cruz-Ferreira (2006), De Houwer (2009, Chapters 5 and 6), Leopold (1970), Ronjat (1913)

BFLA children's sounds in the second year of life

The four books mentioned above, Deuchar & Quay (2000: 29–34), Ingram (1981/82), Johnson & Lancaster (1998), Kehoe (2002), Keshavarz & Ingram (2002), Lleó & Rakow (2005), Schnitzer & Krasinski (1994, 1996)

On the kinds of early words that BFLA children say

Conboy & Thal (2006), David & Li (2005), Holowka *et al.* (2002), Porsché (1983), Qi *et al.* (2006)

The vocabulary spurt in BFLA children

Deuchar & Quay (2000, Table 4.1), Pearson & Fernández (1994), Vila (1984), Wanner (1996)

Numbers of words: differences between:

- **BFLA children**: Conboy & Thal (2006), Marchman *et al.* (2004), Patterson (2000, 2002)

- **a BFLA child's two languages**: David & Li (2003), Nicoladis (1998), Patterson (1999, 2000)

Translation equivalents

David & Li (2008), Deuchar & Quay (2000), Lanvers (1999), Nicoladis (1998), Pearson *et al.* (1995a), Porsché (1983), Qi *et al.* (2006), Quay (1995), Wanner (1996)

4

Making sentences

This chapter explains how BFLA children progress from combining just two words to saying sentences combining two clauses. The focus in this chapter is solely on speaking, but, of course, BFLA children continue to learn to understand more and more words, as well as sentences and their grammatical features.

- The chapter traces the increasing length of BFLA children's utterances.

- It discusses BFLA children's use of mixed utterances.

- It emphasizes that BFLA children's use of mixed utterances is very much determined by how people react to them.

- It explains that BFLA children's unilingual utterances in Language A follow the rules of Language A and that unilingual utterances in Language Alpha follow the rules of Language Alpha. This confirms the Separate Development Hypothesis.

- It shows that BFLA children's two languages can be spoken at similar levels of skill, or at vastly different levels (to the point that some BFLA children say sentences in just a single language).

- It links levels of skill in a language to input factors such as changed frequency of input and people allowing the use of just a single language in conversation.

- ...And shows how BFLA children who speak two languages mostly choose the socially appropriate one.

Again, this chapter zooms in on the four BFLA children you've become acquainted with in the previous chapters. What is described for each child is necessarily selective.

Before you continue, it may be a good idea to reread the sections on each of the four children in Chapter 3.

Lily: World traveller

After she had started saying two-word combinations in Dutch, Lily continued to say single Mandarin words to her mother Xiu. She also continued to say single Dutch words to grandma Rita and to father Hein. These days she spent very little time just with her mother. Rather, when she saw her mother, her father would usually be present as well, and if she said a Dutch word combination, it was either directed at her father, or at both her parents together. Xiu often repeated what Lily said in Mandarin before actually replying to what she had said.

One weekend, two months after she had said her first word combination (in Dutch), Lily surprised Xiu by saying a fully Mandarin word combination: when she was 23 months old, Lily said 'qu4 wan2' (Mandarin for 'go out to play'). She said this while she was getting her coat and boots. Xiu immediately responded by saying in Mandarin: 'sure, we'll go outside if you like!'. After this first Mandarin two-word combination, many others followed.

Occasionally, Lily would put a Mandarin and a Dutch word together, like in 'snoepje yao4'. Here, she put together the Dutch word for 'candy' ('snoepje'), and the Mandarin word for 'want' ('yao4'; notation in Pinyin). These kinds of utterances where words from two languages are combined are called **mixed utterances**.

When Lily said 'snoepje yao4' to Hein, he asked her what she meant. She then repeated her mixed utterance, and Hein said (in Dutch): 'oh, you mean you want a piece of candy! How do I say that?', and Lily then replied in Dutch: 'snoepje hebbe!' (candy have; meaning: I want to have a candy). She then got her candy.

When Lily said a mixed utterance to her mother, Xiu would respond much like Hein. Both Lily's parents, then, were making it clear to her that they didn't really want her to say any mixed utterances, but that they wanted her to speak Dutch to Hein, and Mandarin to Xiu. As such, they were using monolingual discourse strategies (see Chapter 1). Soon, Lily stopped saying mixed utterances pretty much, and most of what she said was now entirely in Dutch, or entirely in Mandarin: she was saying **unilingual utterances** in each.

Lily celebrated her second birthday in the Netherlands, and the people who came to her party included some Chinese friends of Xiu's but mostly they were Dutch-speaking relatives and friends. People marveled at Lily's speaking ability in two languages, and generally thought it was great that such a little girl could make herself understood in two languages. At the party there were also a few little Dutch-speaking children. One of them spoke in much longer sentences than Lily, even though he was two months younger, but the other two, who were slightly older than Lily, said just the same kinds of things as Lily did in Dutch. But, of course, none of them could say anything in Chinese!

Lily's birthday party was, at the same time, a bit of a going away party, because it was time for another visit to China. Because Xiu couldn't take that much time off work, the trip was going to be just three weeks long this time, and Hein was not planning on visiting, even though he would of course miss his family.

When Xiu and Lily arrived in China, Lily was not surprised to hear other people speak Mandarin (as she *had* been a year earlier). She recognized grandma Mei from video phone calls over the Internet and seemed to feel at home right away. Lily no longer spoke any Dutch now. After all, there was nobody to speak it to. After a week of speaking and hearing much more Mandarin than she had done in the Netherlands, Lily started to say somewhat longer little sentences in Mandarin. Aside from two-word combinations, she now also said little sentences with three or four words.

To the family in China, Lily sounded just like any other child her age. In fact, they couldn't believe that Lily also spoke Dutch. Although she didn't sound quite like an adult yet, she showed no obvious trace of a foreign accent.

The time in China was soon over and Lily and Xiu arrived back in the Netherlands. Hein was happy to have them back home. In the week after their return, Lily spent more time with grandma Rita again but early in the mornings, before Xiu had to go to work, there was a lot of video calling with China. Lily and Xiu were still both jet lagged and wide awake at 5 am. As the jet lag subsided, video calls were reserved for the weekends. This all meant that Lily experienced hightened input in Dutch, and heard much less Mandarin.

Lily soon started to say longer Dutch utterances. By the time she was two and a half, she often said perfect little Dutch sentences. These would occasionally have as many as seven or eight words in them. They usually were put in the order you would expect for Dutch.

Lily's Mandarin sentences were generally shorter. Also, she didn't say as many of them, since she spent far more time with speakers of Dutch than with her mother or on the phone to China. Lily did continue to learn many new words in Mandarin, though, because Xiu would make a point of reading a new little book with her every night. She would repeat the new books the week after, and then start with a new set of books for the following week. She had her mother Mei send her new books from China regularly.

Lily's box Adjusting her language use to changing circumstances	
In the Netherlands	*In China*
more Dutch than Mandarin	only Mandarin

Soon after Lily's third birthday, Xiu gave notice at her job. Lily would soon start going to preschool, and Xiu knew that once that started, there would be more restrictions in terms of when Lily could travel. Xiu wanted to take Lily to China for a much longer time this year so she could get better acquainted with her family and her second country. Hein supported the idea fully, but made sure that this time he could visit for a longer time than when Lily was one year old.

Lily and Xiu travelled to China when Lily was 3;2. In China, Lily soon started to say much longer sentences in Mandarin. Like the other two times, Lily only spoke Mandarin in China. Lily's language skills in Mandarin increased by the day. Everyone was amazed she spoke so well. And, again, they couldn't believe that Lily also spoke Dutch.

After five weeks in which Lily had not heard any Dutch, Hein came to visit. When he arrived, Lily understood what he said, but spoke to him in Mandarin! This she had never done before. After a few days, though, she started to say some things to Hein in Dutch again, and after a week she was back to her fluency from before. Sadly, Hein soon had to leave again.

Lily and Xiu stayed in China for another month, during which time Lily's Mandarin improved in leaps and bounds. By age 3;5, when it was time to leave again, Lily was a talkative little girl who could be quite entertaining with her made-up stories about dragons and princesses.

Arno: Racing along

Arno used two-word combinations in each language starting at age 16 months. He didn't stick to these for very long though. At age 18 months he was starting to say many little sentences consisting of three or four words, and soon he no longer said any two-word combinations.

The little sentences Arno said followed the rules of French and German for the order of the words. For instance, in French he would say: 'veux rester ici' (want stay here; I want to stay here), where like in adult French he didn't put any other word in between the verbs 'veux' and 'rester', but in German he would say: 'kann nicht zumachen!' (can not close; I can't close it!), where he did put a word between the verbs 'kann' and 'zumachen', just like it's supposed to be in German.

Arno's short sentences were still lacking a number of things adults would say, like 'je' (I) in 'veux rester ici' and 'ich' (I) and 'es' (it) in 'kann nicht zumachen!', but when he combined French words with each other, the sentence had a French-like structure, and when he combined German words with each other, the sentence had a German-like structure.

When Arno started attending a part-time playgroup, the retired teacher who organized it was impressed with the way Arno spoke French. She said that in her entire teaching career she had never met a child who spoke French that well at such an early age.

Arno's box Real sentences	
In French	
'tu veux jouer avec moi?'	you-want-play-with-me? (do you want to play with me?)
	pronoun-verb-verb-preposition-pronoun
'faut pas casser le camion!'	should-not-break-the-truck (you should not damage the truck)
	verb-adverb-verb-article-noun
In German	
'ich will nicht schlafen gehen!'	I-want-not-sleep-go (I don't want to go to sleep)
	pronoun-verb-adverb-verb-verb
'bitte kannst Du mir helfen?'	please-can-you-me-help (please can you help me?)
	particle-verb-pronoun-pronoun-verb

When he was 21 months of age, Arno started to put many more words into his sentences, regardless of what language he was speaking. He now also said many of the 'little words' of French and German.

When at age two Arno went for a routine check-up to his pediatrician, who did all sorts of developmental tests and also checked on his language development in French, she put him at the 'top of his class' in comparison to other children learning French from birth. The pediatrician didn't realize that Arno spoke German as well. When Bruno came to pick up Alix and Arno, and Arno said hello to him in German, the pediatrician couldn't believe her ears. She didn't realize it was possible for a bilingually raised child to speak so well.

Arno continued to get better and better at speaking his two languages. With people who spoke only one language to him he spoke that one, too, as he had done earlier. With people who spoke two languages with him, he continued to do so as well, but now there seemed to be some kind of pattern emerging. He preferred to talk about his toys and trucks in German, but when he wanted something to eat or drink, he used French. When his parents came to think about it, they realized they had similar divisions between their two languages, and that they tended to speak German when they played with Arno or talked to him about his toys and trucks.

Occasionally, Arno said a sentence in French that had a single German word in it. An example is 'mais où est le Hund?' (but where is the dog?; everything here is in French except the German noun 'Hund', dog). Arno said this while he was rummaging through his box of small toy animals, looking for the dog. Such mixed utterances were quite rare in Arno's speech, though, and if overheard by one of his parents Arno would be asked to say the whole sentence in French or German, and not both. Arno was happy to oblige, and could easily modify his sentence.

Mixed utterances only very occasionally appeared in the speech of the adults around Arno, and if anyone said a mixed utterance, their conversational partner would point it out to them. Arno's family had nothing against mixed utterances, and Alix and Bruno had used them frequently before Arno was born, but they had decided they wanted Arno to learn French that was as 'French' as possible, and German that was as 'German' as possible. They didn't want him complaining when he grew up that he hadn't had the chance to 'properly' learn two languages.

By the time Arno was two and a half years old, he said complex sentences in both languages. Those are big sentences that consist of at least two smaller ones (clauses). For instance, Arno said: 'quand je suis grand je veux être pompier' (French for 'when I'm big/I want to be a fireman'; the slash indicates where one clause stops and another one starts). A German example is: 'was kommt wenn die Leute böse sind?' (what comes/when the people are angry?; with 'comes' Arno probably meant 'happens').

Even though Arno was often sounding fairly mature in the sorts of ideas and structures he expressed, his speech sounds still gave him away as a little boy. He was still using quite a few phonological processes, and whenever he visited his relatives in Germany they first needed a few hours to get used to how he talked. But once they knew what sounds he usually deleted or substituted, they understood him perfectly well.

Ramon: Saying sentences in two languages

The pattern that started with Ramon first saying two-word combinations in English and only later in Spanish continued in the sense that he said many more two-word combinations in English than in Spanish. You would think that since he heard about equal amounts of both languages there wouldn't be such a large difference. The thing is, when he was taken care of by his grandma Rosa, he heard a lot of Spanish sentences with English words thrown in. These were mostly nouns borrowed from English. When he was at grandma's, Ramon also used a lot of two-word combinations with an English and a Spanish word in them. In addition to unilingual utterances in English and Spanish, then, Ramon said a fair number of mixed utterances. He did not use these at the day-care center, and only rarely at home with his parents.

Grandma Rosa didn't mind that Ramon said mixed utterances and thus used English words when he spoke to her. To the contrary, she was proud that her grandson knew English and bragged about it to her friends. Rosa did not insist on Ramon speaking just Spanish. Rather, she encouraged him in his use of English words by repeating them in English. She was certainly not using any monolingual discourse strategies. Instead, she was using bilingual discourse strategies.

On the whole, about half of Ramon's two-word combinations were entirely in English, a quarter entirely in Spanish, and the other quarter were mixed.

This pattern continued as Ramon started to build longer sentences consisting of three or four words. These appeared in his speech soon after his second birthday. When Ramon was at the day-care center, he would speak only English. At grandma's, he used mostly Spanish, but every second sentence had an English word thrown in. That was usually a noun, such as 'bowling', 'TV', or 'hamburger'.

At home with Julia and Alan, Ramon tended to speak Spanish to his mother when he meant to talk only to her. In this, he took the lead from Julia's example. Whereas earlier, Julia had spoken Spanish to Ramon only when his father was not in the same room, she had gradually started to speak more Spanish to Ramon. Alan didn't mind, since the topics that Julia discussed with Ramon in Spanish didn't really concern him. For instance, when Julia asked Ramon what he wanted to drink, this would be in Spanish. Also, with the increased presence of Spanish in the house, Alan had learned to understand more Spanish and certainly did not feel left out. Julia would switch to English when the topic did involve Alan. For instance, when she told Ramon to put on his shoes to go out for a walk she would say so in English if Alan was coming along on the walk. But if Alan was staying at home, she would use Spanish to ask Ramon to put on his shoes.

Only very occasionally did Ramon say a word in English when he spoke exclusively to his mother. He would do this hesitatingly, and Julia would always tell him what the English word was in Spanish, and then he would repeat the sentence in Spanish. In furnishing the Spanish words, Julia was using monolingual discourse strategies. When Ramon meant to address just his father, he spoke only English. In talking to both his parents at once, Ramon also spoke English. His mother would then respond in English. Ramon's use of mixed utterances was more or less reserved for the time he spent with grandma Rosa.

Ramon's box Ramon's language repertoire and language choice	
His repertoire	**His language choice**
Unilingual utterances	
English	• used at the day-care center
	• used to address his father
	• used to address both his parents
Spanish	• used to address his mother
Mixed utterances	• used to address his grandma Rosa and her friends

By the time he was two and a half, Ramon started to spend much less time with grandma. She had developed a health problem that tired her greatly, and she could spend only a few hours each week taking care of Ramon. She was very sorry about it but that's how it had to be. This meant that Ramon now spent a lot more time at the day-care center.

At age 2;7, Ramon started to say longer sentences in English. These now routinely contained six or seven words. His Spanish lagged behind a bit, in the sense that Ramon's Spanish utterances had a maximum of four or five words usually. Ramon now also knew a lot more words in English than in Spanish. His mother tried to make a point of reading Spanish books to him every night to help with his Spanish vocabulary, but often she was too tired, or Ramon was too tired. He did not particularly like reading books. He much preferred to play with his building blocks before going to sleep. Julia and Alan agreed that he probably just needed some quiet time by himself after a busy day with the other children at the day-care center. Book reading became an activity for the weekend only.

By the time of his third birthday, Ramon sounded like any other child in his day-care center. Like many of the other three-year-olds there, he now had a very pronounced American twang in his speech when he spoke English. Luckily, his Spanish didn't have any of that! Rather, his Spanish sounded like that of other bilingual children in the area who were learning English and Spanish from early on, and started to resemble the kind of Spanish the adults spoke around him (mostly his mother and his grandma). Their Spanish was no longer like the Spanish of people who had only lived in Mexico though. The fact that they all knew some English and had lived away from Mexico for a long time meant that their accent had changed a bit. The way Ramon spoke Spanish reflected this kind of Mexican–American accent.

Toshie: Catching up

Toshie's two-word combinations were all in Japanese. In addition, except for some words for Korean foods, Toshie no longer said any words in Korean, although her mother Yun continued to speak to her in Korean when no one else was present. Yun was thinking of perhaps going back to work, but she realized that if she did, Toshie would hear far less Korean, and the chance that Toshie would ever speak Korean would be even lower. Yun didn't know what to do.

At the age of 2;3, Toshie started to say much longer sentences in Japanese. In fact, there was quite a sudden difference between Toshie's earlier two-word combinations and the seemingly perfect little Japanese sentences she now said. Toshie's father and grandparents praised her for speaking so well, and Yun was happy about it too, but started to feel rejected by Toshie's lack of Korean. Yun decided that it was quite important to her that Toshie spoke Korean, and also she considered that maybe when Toshie was older she would be unhappy if she could not speak Korean, and blame her mother.

Yun thought about how she might turn things around. Increasing the amount of Korean that Toshie heard by talking Korean to Toshie around her father and grandparents was out of the question. Reading even more books in Korean was difficult, since Yun already was reading so many Korean books with Toshie. Toshie loved that and understood a lot, but didn't respond in Korean. Perhaps if Yun started to pretend not to understand Toshie's Japanese if they were alone? Yun decided to try that in a gentle way.

When Toshie asked Yun in Japanese to read a book with her, Yun asked her in Korean: 'you want to read a book? is that what you want?'. When Toshie answered affirmatively, Yun then said in Korean: 'say how mommy says it: please I would like to read a book mommy'. Toshie was dumbstruck. This had never happened before. Toshie softly repeated in Japanese that she wanted to read a book. Yun then asked her: 'what is it you want to read?'. Toshie thought for a moment and then said very hesitatingly and so softly that Yun could hardly hear it: 'book'. Toshie said this in Japanese though. Yun was disappointed but repeated Toshie's Japanese word for 'book' in Korean. She then brought out a new book and started to read from it for Toshie.

Yun tried a similar tactic several times afterwards but it seemed impossible to get Toshie to say anything in Korean. In the meantime, Toshie's Japanese blossomed and she was saying sentences that contained two clauses. All Toshie's sentences were pronounced very deliberately and were clearly articulated. Mistakes were rare. Toshie was two and a half.

Yun started to think that Toshie didn't want to try any Korean because she was such a perfectionist and didn't want to say anything wrong. Yun became more and more convinced of this, and concluded that there was nothing she could do about it, and that Toshie would only speak Korean once she, Toshie, decided to do so. After a few months, Yun gave up her futile attempts to get Toshie to speak Korean.

Yun felt that somehow she had let herself down, and needed something to take away her attention from what she considered her failure as a mother to get her child to speak her own language. She decided to accept a job offer she had recently received, and started working part-time when Toshie was 2;7. Toshie stayed home with the grandparents while Yun and father Atsuo were at work.

Toshie's Japanese continued to flourish. It was now only in the few hours per week that she spent alone with her mother that Toshie heard Korean. She continued to understand her mother, but often there were now words she didn't understand. When she asked for clarification, her mother would translate into Japanese. Yun made an effort to make Toshie interested in Korea, but without actual visits there or anyone there that they knew it was hard to teach a little girl about some distant country. Yun came to doubt herself in her desire to transmit her language to her child. After all, had she not turned away from Korea and cut off all her contacts there? What, in fact, was the point even in teaching Toshie Korean? But when Yun thought of giving up speaking Korean to Toshie, she shuddered. No, that she could not. As time went by, Yun stopped worrying about Toshie not speaking any Korean, and was just happy that she could speak so well in Japanese. Yun continued to speak to Toshie in Korean, and Toshie answered in Japanese.

Toshie was now three years old and nothing like the difficult child she had been as a baby. She spoke Japanese just like the other three-year-olds in the neighborhood, except that she seemed to articulate better.

Toshie's box Some examples of sentences at age three

I don't like going to the doctor's

what happens if they eat bad food?

mommy please read me a book

All Japanese utterances rendered in English

Key points: Word combinations become real sentences

- By the time of their second birthday, most BFLA children will be combining two words with each other. This greatly increases their power of expression compared to saying just single words. But in order to communicate more complex ideas, BFLA children need to start putting many more words together to form real sentences that adults will understand.

- Generally, the longer children's utterances become, the higher their skills are in a particular language. Like MFLA children, when BFLA children first start to combine more than two words with each other, they typically do not yet speak in the 'full', 'complete' forms required by their input language(s). Their early multiword utterances often seem to show 'gaps'. For instance, for Arno's 'kann nicht zumachen!' (see earlier), you could easily think that this was an attempt at the sentence 'ich kann es nicht zumachen' (I-can-it-not-close), with the underlined 'little bits' simply left out. The 'little bits' here are the pronouns 'ich' and 'es' (I and it), but they could be articles or prepositions, or many other words or parts of words that help to structure a sentence. Indeed, many of young children's early sentences sound funny because they lack those 'little bits'.

- Just like MFLA children, BFLA children gradually say longer utterances as they get older. These longer utterances have increasingly more of the important 'little bits' in them and sound more and more like the sentences adults would say. In the fourth year of life, BFLA children start to be able to say complex sentences that combine two or three clauses, as in Ramon's 'if I paint this like this can I do another one?', where the first clause starts with 'if' and the second one with 'can'.

- Like MFLA children, BFLA children differ from each other in the ages at which they first start to combine more than two words into sentences, start to say even longer and complex utterances with more of the required 'little bits', and start to say complex sentences. BFLA children don't necessarily do any of this for both of their languages at once though. You can see this in the Variation box below. It shows the ages for each language at which each of this book's four main characters started saying three- or four-word combinations, six- or seven-word combinations and complex sentences. Some of the information in the box summarizes what I wrote earlier, while other information is new.

Variation box Different timings for major developments in the second year			
What?	Child	Language A	Language Alpha
the first combination of 3 or 4 words	Lily	2;3	2;1
	Arno	1;6	1;6
	Ramon	2;2	2;2
	Toshie	2;3	n.a.
the first combination of 6 or 7 words	Lily	2;6	3;3
	Arno	1;9	1;9
	Ramon	2;7	2;11
	Toshie	2;4	n.a.
the first complex sentence	Lily	2;11	3;3
	Arno	2;6	2;6
	Ramon	3;0	3;4
	Toshie	2;6	n.a.

n.a. = not applicable

- You can see from the box that Arno continues the trend he set earlier: he is developing much faster than the other three children, and his two languages are developing at the same pace. Toshie is no longer the slowest developer, as she was earlier. Instead, she is rapidly catching up with Arno-the-speedy-one. Unlike Arno, Toshie is developing in just one language though (at least, as far as speaking is concerned).

- Ramon and Lily are somewhere in between. By their third birthday, they both are more skilled in one language than in the other. This means they both have a **weaker** and a **stronger language**. For Lily, the difference between her two languages is much more pronounced than it is for Ramon. In her Language A, Dutch, Lily is saying complex sentences whereas in her Language Alpha, Mandarin, she sounds much more immature, since she is just saying sentences with four or five words. It looks as if her development in Mandarin has stagnated. But with the trip to China at age 3;2 this changes, and Lily makes rapid gains in Mandarin. However, she no longer has any need to speak Dutch. In fact, when there is a renewed need for Dutch (with Hein's visit), Lily has to relearn Dutch! There is a temporary reversal, then, in which language is Lily's stronger one and which is her weaker one.

- Ramon isn't experiencing the strong changes in his linguistic environment that word-traveller Lily is. His Language A is more constantly the stronger one.

- The fact that BFLA children's two languages may develop at very different rates shows that each language follows its own developmental route. Furthermore, BFLA children's unilingual utterances show grammatical characteristics that are typical of just a single language. That is, when BFLA children say utterances with words from just Language A, they will generally use the word order and the 'little bits' that are typical of Language A, rather than Language Alpha. The same applies the other way round: utterances in Language Alpha use the word order and 'little bits' of Language Alpha. What this means is that BFLA children develop the grammatical structures of their two languages independently of each other. This generalization is known as the **Separate Development Hypothesis** or **SDH**.

- The question is whether BFLA children's sounds also develop separately in each language. Because of young children's use of phonological processes and their general articulatory immaturity, this is hard to say. However, BFLA children who are mature enough to be saying unilingual sentences consisting of more than four words usually have no clear accent that could give away the fact that they also speak another language (Lily, Arno, Ramon). BFLA children who speak just a single language have no 'foreign' accent in that language either (Toshie).

- Some BFLA children say a fair number of mixed utterances once they are able to say three- or four-word combinations, but others do not. Mixed utterances contain words from two languages. The extent to which BFLA children will use mixed utterances very much depends on how the people around them react to them. They may want children to speak just unilingual utterances, and may help children do this by offering them the translation equivalent for a particular word (Lily, Arno). Alternatively, people may not care whether children use mixed utterances or even encourage their use (Ramon).

- Young BFLA children in the third year of life are able to respond as expected to people's expectations about which language to use when. Many will tend to respond in the language they are spoken to (Lily, Arno, Ramon). When BFLA children are the ones to start up a conversation, they will use the language that they usually speak to a particular person (Lily). If they are used to speaking two languages to a particular person they will choose the language that fits the context (Ramon) or the topic (Arno). In contrast, BFLA children who were used to speaking mainly one language when they were younger may now speak nothing else (Toshie). It may be very hard to change that pattern (Toshie).

Activities and discussion points

1. This activity is the basis for a class discussion. Divide the class (if relevant) into two parts: students who speak just a single language, and students who speak more than just a single language:

   (a) if you speak just a single language: on a scale from 1 to 10, how well do you speak it? Do you speak it better or worse than other people you know who speak only that same language? Do you think you speak it better than people who have stopped going to school at age 16 or so? And what does 'speaking better or worse' mean to you?

   (b) if you speak more than just a single language: do you speak these two languages equally well?

      • if your answer is 'yes', explain what makes you say so. And why do you think you speak the two languages equally well?

      • if your answer is 'no', explain what makes you say so. And why do you think you do not speak the two languages equally well?

2. Find a family with a BFLA child who is between 2;6 and 3;6 and who is learning at least one language that you speak and understand. Ask whether you can make an audio recording of you playing with the child for an hour using the child's own toys. It's fine if the parents are in the room during the recording. Explain that you are studying child language development.

   Once you get the OK, make your recording (but give the child a few minutes to get acquainted with you first). I suggest you bring an attractive age-appropriate children's book that you can use during the session to elicit speech from the child. You can then give this book to the child afterwards as a gift. Play with the child but try to elicit as much speech from him/her as you can.

   When you get back home, listen to the recording and write down:

   (a) what language(s) the child spoke

   (b) what language(s) you spoke

   (c) whether you could mostly understand the child

   (d) the longest utterance you heard the child say

   (e) any mixed utterances the child might have said

   (f) anything else that struck you as interesting

3. Re-read all the information about Lily and Ramon in Chapters 3 and 4. Summarize the steps in their spoken language development on two pages, arranged in age periods of six months. Focus on the kinds of things they said, on the language(s) they said them in and on any changes in their linguistic environments. Do you see any patterns emerge? How are they similar or different for both children?

Further reading

BFLA children's sounds in the third and fourth year of life:

- **their use of intonation at the word or sentence level:** Brulard & Carr (2003), Gut (2000a), Paradis (2001), Lleó *et al.* (2007)

- **their use of separate speech segments:** Lleó & Rakow (2005), Pearson *et al.* (1995b), Pearson & Navarro (1996), Ronjat (1913), Schnitzer & Krasinski (1994, 1996)

- **no foreign accent:** Johnson & Wilson (2002)

The gradual progression from two-word combinations to complex sentences

De Houwer (2009, Chapter 7)

BFLA children develop two separate grammatical systems

Almgren & Barreña (2000), Bonnesen (2008), De Houwer (1990, 2005, 2009, Chapter 7), Meisel (2001), Nicoladis (1999), Paradis & Genesee (1996), Salustri & Hyams (2006), Serratrice (2001, 2002), Silva-Corvalán & Sánchez-Walker (2007), Sinka & Schelletter (1998)

BFLA children's two languages may or may not develop at the same rate:

- **developing at about the same rate:** De Houwer (1990), Hulk & Müller (2000), Meisel (1990), Müller (1990), Ronjat (1913), Silva-Corvalán & Sánchez-Walker (2007)

- **not developing at the same rate:** Bernardini (2003), Jisa (1995), Juan-Garau & Pérez-Vidal (2000), Leopold (1970), Müller & Kupisch (2003), Qi (2005), Schlyter (1995)

Structural features of BFLA children's mixed utterances combining more than two words

Cantone (2007), De Houwer (1990, 1995), Radford *et al.* (2007), Paradis *et al.* (2000), Sinka (2000)

Factors explaining why BFLA children's sentences are mixed or unilingual in Language A or Language Alpha

Allen *et al.* (2002), De Houwer (1990), Goodz (1989), Jisa (2000), Lanza (1992, 1997), Mishina (1999)

Big changes in the input have an immediate effect on BFLA children's language use and skill

De Houwer (2009, Chapter 4), Gut (2000b), Jisa (2000), Kupisch (2003), Lanza (1998), Leopold (1970), Ronjat (1913), von Raffler-Engel (1965)

5

Preschool and beyond

This chapter concludes the overview of the major developments in BFLA children's language use up until the point that they are old enough to start to learn to read and write.

- Its focus is on BFLA children of preschool age and just a bit older.

- It explains how there continues to be an important influence of BFLA children's language environments on how well they speak and on what language(s) they speak.

- It discusses BFLA children's use of mixed utterances.

- It explains how BFLA children are able to repair their utterances.

- It again shows that BFLA children's two languages can be spoken at similar levels of skill, or at vastly different levels (to the point that some BFLA children speak just a single language).

- It shows the big importance of preschool, school and professionals such as teachers and school counselors.

For the last time, this chapter zooms in on the four BFLA children Lily, Arno, Ramon and Toshie. Again, what is described for each child is selective.

Before you continue, it may be a good idea to re-read the sections on each of the four children in Chapter 4.

Lily: Storyteller

On the plane back to the Netherlands after the long trip to China, Lily was chattering away in Mandarin so much that sometimes Xiu wished she would just be quiet for a little while. Xiu got her wish when after passing through customs Lily saw Hein. Lily flew into her father's arms and smiled a lot and gave him lots of kisses but did not say anything! This was reminiscent of what she had done earlier when Hein had come to visit in China. Unlike then, Hein and Xiu didn't worry about it now, because they were sure that after a few days, Lily's Dutch would come back, just as it had before.

And indeed it did! The first few days, Lily said a few Dutch words very hesitantly. But when she got encouragement she became braver, and grandma Rita and father Hein were happy to hear Lily say Dutch sentences once again.

Lily did stutter a bit in Dutch, though. She also started stuttering a bit in Mandarin. This lasted a few weeks. It seemed as if Lily was trying to say much more complicated ideas than she was able to, and this made her stutter. Grandma Rita knew from experience that it was common for children between three and a half and five to stutter, especially if they were trying to say very long sentences.

At age four, Lily started attending preschool. She was no longer stuttering in either Dutch or Mandarin. She was quite entertaining when she told her fantastic stories about princesses and knights (no more dragons!). At school, her stories made her very popular with the other children. Her stories didn't always have a good ending, but they started off very well, and the twists in the story line were very amusing. The preschool teacher marvelled at Lily's storytelling ability. She would expect older children to be able to tell stories like Lily's. Maybe Lily's storytelling skills had been inspired and fostered by grandma Mei in China, who had told Lily many different stories every day and had encouraged her to tell stories too.

Grandma Mei came to visit when Lily was four and a half. This allowed Hein and Xiu to take their first vacation without Lily, and Lily was very happy to have grandma Mei's full attention. With all the stories that grandma Mei told her, Lily's Mandarin vocabulary and storytelling abilities increased in leaps and bounds.

By the time Lily was six years old the preschool teacher certified that Lily was ready to go to school, and that her Dutch was better developed than expected for a child her age. She also wrote that Lily had a very vivid imagination and told wonderful stories. The fact that Lily also spoke Mandarin wasn't something the teacher was very aware of. Lily spoke Mandarin fluently, but as before, her skill in Mandarin greatly increased when she was in China or when grandma Mei came to visit, but decreased at other times. Xiu wanted Lily to learn to write in Chinese, but decided together with Hein to give Lily the time to learn to write in Dutch first.

Arno: The school counselor making trouble

At the age of three, Arno was speaking both German and French pretty well. He was building complex sentences in both languages. His speech sounds were still a bit different from adult ones, but his use of phonological processes was gradually diminishing to give way to the adult forms of words.

Arno started attending a bilingual German–French preschool soon after his third birthday. A German-speaking teacher was responsible for Mondays to Wednesdays, and on Thursdays and Fridays a French-speaking teacher took over. Many of the children in the school were raised with German and French, just like Arno. The children soon learned to speak just German when the German-speaking teacher was in the school, and French when the French-speaking teacher was around. The children even switched languages in speaking to each other, so that they started off the week in German and switched to French on Thursdays, when they saw the French-speaking teacher.

Both the German-speaking and the French-speaking teacher took care not to say any mixed utterances, and when any of the children said a mixed utterance they asked them what they meant. The children usually responded by changing their mixed utterance into a unilingual one. For instance, Arno once said to the German-speaking teacher: 'ich kann mein sac nicht aufmachen!' (I-can-my-bag-not-open), using a French words ('sac') in an otherwise completely German utterance. The teacher asked him in German what he meant. Arno then repeated in perfect German: 'Meine Tasche! Ich kann meine Tasche nicht aufmachen!' (my-bag! I-can-my-bag-not-open). The teacher then went over to see how she could help. It turned out that the lock on the bag no longer worked.

In changing from a mixed utterance to a unilingual utterance expressing the same thing, Arno was **repairing** his original utterance. That is, he was making its form more appropriate. In this case, the form had to do with his choice of language. Arno was also able to repair his unilingual utterances. For instance, when he came home from preschool he said to his mother in French: 'mon sac est tombé'. His mother asked in disbelief: 'tombé?' (fell down?). Arno was carrying his bag. Arno then quickly said: 'non, mon sac est cassé.' (no-my-bag-is-broken). He here repaired his choice of words within the same language.

When he was four, Arno started to be able to tell a little story, but often it didn't make much sense. He got better and better, though, and by age five he was attempting to tell jokes. He had certainly learned what you need in a joke, but rather than being funny, his jokes tended to be shaggy dog stories. Yet, Arno's parents were nice enough to laugh when he had finished telling yet another 'joke'.

By age six, Arno and his family moved to Germany. This was a big change for everyone, but luckily Arno was able to speak German and start going to school in Germany. Like the other children, Arno soon learned to read in German. His parents wanted him to learn to read in French too. They thought it would be a pity if Arno's equal and good skills in both languages were to change into a situation where one of the languages became 'the underdog', especially since they weren't sure how long their jobs would keep them in Germany.

However, Arno's parents weren't sure whether it was a good idea to start teaching Arno to read in French when he was only in his first year of learning to read in German. They decided to consult the school educational counselor. Much to their consternation, the counselor expressed great concerns over the fact that Arno spoke two languages. She sternly said that speaking two languages was bad for young children, and surely Arno belonged in a school for special education that looked after handicapped children. She said she would start the procedure to transfer Arno to such a school. Arno's parents tried to explain that Arno was doing very well, and had no problems at all because of speaking two languages, and that he was reading German at the same level as most of the children in his class. The counselor dismissed all this as being impossible. She just wouldn't listen.

When, after the visit to the school counselor, Arno's parents started receiving letters from the school recommending that Arno start going to a school for special education, they decided to look for other regular schools in the area that would accept Arno's bilingualism. Luckily, the teachers, director and school counselor in the primary school of the next village welcomed the fact that Arno spoke two languages and thought it was wonderful that Arno would be able to perhaps later teach the other children some French. Arno was sad to have to leave the school where he had already made some friends, but being the easy-going child he was, he adjusted well to the new school and soon had friends there too.

Ramon: Big translator

By age 3;6, Ramon was saying complex sentences in both Spanish and English. His Spanish vocabulary was not quite as developed as his English vocabulary though. Often, Ramon seemed to be using a mixed utterance instead of a fully Spanish one when he didn't know a particular word in Spanish, as in 'no sé donde están mis boots' (not-I know-where-are-my-boots; I don't know where my boots are), where the English word 'boots' appears in a Spanish sentence. The words he didn't know were usually nouns, but there were verbs and adjectives, too, that he didn't know in Spanish but only in English.

As before, Ramon's grandma didn't mind his use of mixed utterances and didn't necessarily respond by telling him the Spanish word, but Ramon's mother Julia tried to tell him the Spanish word whenever she noticed that Ramon was saying a mixed utterance. Often, though, she didn't notice and so didn't comment on Ramon's mixed utterance. When Ramon was at the English-speaking day-care center or talked to his father Alan he never used mixed utterances but only spoke English.

As Ramon got older, he seemed to be using more and more mixed utterances, and fewer Spanish utterances. His mother soon got tired of always trying to stop him in his tracks and tell Ramon the word in Spanish that he had said in English. She did realize, though, that this way soon Ramon wouldn't progress much in Spanish, and might even stop speaking it altogether. She didn't want this to happen.

Ramon's parents decided to enroll Ramon in a bilingual preschool so that he would have more need to speak Spanish. They found one that was not too far away. For Ramon it was a big change. He really liked the preschool teacher, though, and soon made new friends.

At the school, there was no clear separation between the languages. The students were allowed to speak either English or Spanish, and mixed utterances were also allowed. The teacher herself used mostly Spanish, but spoke some English too. She occasionally used mixed utterances as well. Ramon was very excited when his grandma Rosa was invited to the school to teach the children Mexican songs.

With some friends who spoke little English, Ramon started to speak Spanish. He loved serving as a translator between his friends and the teacher, even though the teacher understood both English and Spanish. Translating soon became a favorite kind of game for Ramon, and the teacher was happy to use Ramon as a helping hand in the classroom to teach words in the other language to new children who arrived at school knowing only English or Spanish.

Soon, Ramon was using a lot more Spanish than before. By the age of 4;6, Ramon was telling stories in Spanish and English. He continued to say mixed utterances, but they were far less common now than just before he started to attend the preschool. When he now did use mixed utterances, the reason was not that he didn't know the Spanish translation of an English word. Rather, his mixed utterances now seemed to be more like slips of the tongue, and when Ramon now said a mixed utterance he often would repeat the utterance just in Spanish.

Ramon now was highly aware of what language he was speaking, what languages other people spoke, whether they spoke them well, whether they also knew another language and whether they liked mixed utterances. He talked about all this with his parents. He also noticed how in Spanish television programs there were quite a few English words said with a Spanish accent, but how in English television programs there were hardly any Spanish words. Ramon watched Sesame Street on television both in Spanish and in English, and was fascinated by letters.

At age five, Ramon was able to read a lot of words in Spanish and English that he saw on cereal boxes, magazine covers, signs on doors and so forth. He seemed ready for a 'real' school. His parents enrolled him at a public English-speaking primary school that had an optional Spanish program. This way, Ramon would get a good basis in English but also progress in Spanish.

Two weeks after Ramon had started at the school, the Spanish program he had enrolled in was cancelled. The teacher had taken ill, and there was no replacement available. Alan and Julia decided to keep Ramon at the school in spite of this setback.

When Ramon got home from school, he started to talk to Julia in English more and more. At first, Julia didn't mind. She wanted to hear Ramon's school stories and responded to him in Spanish when he spoke to her in English. But gradually, Ramon seemed to be having real problems speaking Spanish after he got home from school. He was in an English-speaking environment all day (he now was at school for all sorts of extracurricular activities, too), and it just seemed too much of an effort for him to speak Spanish. Ramon did continue to understand Spanish though. Julia was just starting to despair when the Spanish program at the school took off again. After a few weeks in the program, Ramon was again speaking more Spanish.

Toshie: Slowly starting to speak Language Alpha

Toshie continued to get better and better in Japanese. At preschool, she was among the more talkative children and she learned to tell stories. Yun was proud of Toshie's development, especially considering that she had had such a late start in starting to talk.

Yun got used to the fact that Toshie never spoke to her in Korean. Toshie did continue to understand Korean, but as before, Yun occasionally had to explain a word or an expression that she had said in Korean.

At age six, Toshie entered first grade and started to learn to read and write in Japanese. At home, Yun taught Toshie to write her name in Korean, but apart from that and the Korean children's books Yun still read to Toshie, Toshie's contacts with written language were in Japanese only.

In the second year of primary school, a new child arrived at school. The boy, Dong, was from Korea and knew no Japanese whatsoever. The schoolteacher knew that Toshie was half Korean and thought she must speak Korean. That's why she asked Toshie to explain a few things to Dong in Korean to help him understand a few important things. Toshie felt embarrassed that she had to tell the teacher she spoke no Korean. The teacher was surprised, but there was nothing she could do.

Dong did not speak at school and didn't know that Toshie understood Korean. However, when Dong heard Yun speak Korean to Toshie when she came to pick her up, he started talking to Toshie. For a moment, Toshie didn't know what to do, but then, very quietly, she said to Dong *in Korean* that the next day she would try to help him. Yun couldn't believe her ears! She was overjoyed, and said to Toshie that she hoped she would start to speak Korean to her too.

The next day at school, Toshie acted as a translator between Dong and the teacher, and said a few things to Dong in rudimentary Korean. She explained to the teacher that she knew just a little bit of Korean. Anyway, it was a start, and Dong felt much better at school now that he had someone who could understand him and who he could understand.

At home, though, Toshie continued to speak Japanese to her mother.

Key points: Consolidating and expanding

- By the time they are attending preschool, children are much more intelligible than earlier, but they still have a way to go until they sound like adults (Lily, Arno, Ramon, Toshie). For many languages, it may take children (whether BFLA or MFLA) up to five years or more to learn to say all the important sounds of their language(s).

- Like for the sound system, BFLA children consolidate their earlier knowledge about words and how to make sentences as they get older. They continue to learn many more new words that they now can use in structures that are even larger than sentences: BFLA children learn to tell stories. These combine several sentences with each other. At first, BFLA children's stories are not that great yet (Arno), but they soon becoming entertaining and fun (Lily).

- Some BFLA children increase their use of mixed utterances (Ramon), while others decrease their use (Arno; Ramon later). Like before, BFLA children's use of mixed utterances depends on whether their conversational partners allow their use or not. Their use may also depend on BFLA children's vocabulary (or lack of it – Ramon). Another reason for children's greater or lesser use of mixed utterances lies in the frequency with which they hear them in their language input. The less children hear them, the less they may use them themselves (Lily, Arno). After all, children want to speak like the people around them.

- The use of mixed utterances may be something that BFLA children can control quite consciously, and are able to change (repair) on an utterance-by-utterance basis (Arno). BFLA children may also be able to translate on demand (Ramon, Toshie). Much depends on how high children's awareness of language and language use is. While such an awareness is present at some level in younger BFLA children, it is during the preschool period that it really takes off.

- As before, BFLA children of preschool age may speak each of their languages with variable skill. Their skill in each may, to a large degree, depend on how often they need to speak a particular language, and on how often they hear it spoken. Changes in BFLA children's language input often lead to quite immediate and noticeable changes in their language use (Lily, Ramon). BFLA children who spoke only a single Language A as toddlers may eventually start to speak Language Alpha as well, at least in circumstances where they feel there is a real need (Toshie).

- As before, there are large differences between preschool BFLA children. Some speak Language A all the time, others much less so. The same goes for Language Alpha. Some have a fairly large proportion of mixed utterances, others not. The Variation box below shows the proportions of use of unilingual utterances in Language A and Language Alpha and mixed utterances for our four BFLA children at the age of five years.

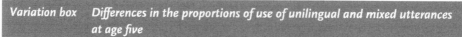

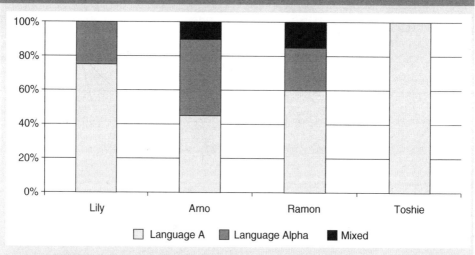

Variation box *Differences in the proportions of use of unilingual and mixed utterances at age five*

- When BFLA children start to go to preschool or school, they will often come back from school filled with stories that they want to tell mom and dad. Because they have spent a whole day in just Language A, BFLA children may not switch back to the language that they usually spoke with mom or dad before (Ramon). This may result in dilingual conversations. If those dilingual conversations become a habit, BFLA children may soon lose their speaking ability in Language Alpha (Toshie earlier).

- Another thing that happens a lot when BFLA children start attending preschool or school is that teachers or educational counselors express negative attitudes about bilingualism (Arno). This may negatively impact on children's development. Fortunately, there are also many schools that value and foster bilingualism (Lily, Arno later, Ramon, Toshie)!

Activities and discussion points

1. Listen to Alicia, a four-year-old Spanish–English bilingual girl, trying to say r's in isolated words in Spanish: http://soe.ku.edu/faculty/gonzalez/ArticulatoryEvolution. php. Notice just how different these r's are from English. You can also hear Alicia speak spontaneously in Spanish via http://soe.ku.edu/faculty/gonzalez/Sounds/ Sounds5/cuento2.wav (website under the direction of Dr Manuela González-Bueno at the University of Kansas, United States of America).

2. Try to gain access to a gregarious BFLA child between the ages of 3;6 and five who you share one language with. Ask the parents if you can come and play with the child for an hour or so. Bring some interesting age-appropriate toys to the appointment. Make a recording of the interaction as you play with the child (preferably, without any one else in the room). Talk your overlapping language with the child (Language A). Afterwards, do one of the activities (or take more than one) listed below.

(a) Listen to the recordings a few times. Did the child talk the way you would expect a child his or her age to sound? Are there any strange or funny things that the child said? Do they just sound 'child-like' or do you think something else is going on? For utterances in Language A: do you hear anything that sounds like there might be an influence from Language Alpha?

(b) Draw up a sheet with three columns: one for unilingual utterances in Language A, one for unilingual utterances in Language Alpha and one for mixed utterances. While you listen to the recording, put a mark in the appropriate column for each utterance the child said. Then count all your marks in each column, calculate the total and the proportion of utterances in each column. Is this child more like Lily, Arno, Ramon or Toshie? For the mixed utterances and the unilingual utterances in Language Alpha (if there are any): what do you think triggered them? Is it anything you said or did? Was there a change of topic? Did someone call out to the child from another room?

3. Re-read the information about Arno in Chapters 3 and 5. How is what Arno is doing in each age period similar or different? Focus on the kinds of things he says and on whether he is using unilingual utterances in each language or mixed utterances (and in what circumstances). Does Arno's language use in Chapter 5 surprise you, or does it seem to be a continuation of what he was doing earlier?

Further reading

BFLA children's development of sounds in the preschool years

González-Bueno (2005), Johnson & Wilson (2002), Schnitzer & Krasinski (1994, 1996)

BFLA children's use of mixed utterances may reflect the relative number of mixed utterances they hear around them

Allen *et al.* (2002), De Houwer (2009, Chapter 4)

BFLA children's stories

Álvarez (1999, 2003, 2008), Lanza (2001), Schlyter (1996), Schneider (1999), Serratrice (2007), Silva-Corvalán (2003)

BFLA children can repair their utterances if they have used the 'wrong' language or a mixed utterance

Comeau *et al.* (1997, 2007), Comeau & Genesee (2001), De Houwer (1990, Chapter 10)

Changes in BFLA children's language input affect what language they will speak and can lead to (temporary) language loss or increased skill

see 'Further reading' in Chapter 4 and Berman (1979), David & Li (2008)

The role of school in continuing to speak a particular language

De Houwer (2009, Chapter 4)

6

In conclusion: Bilingual learning in context

This short chapter concludes the book. In doing so, it focuses on the larger issue of the importance of ideas about bilingualism and bilingual development. It also zooms in on the extra parental work that may be involved in raising bilingual children. In addition, it looks at the variations in children's bilingual environments that can explain much of the variation we see in BFLA children's patterns of language use.

All these aspects pertain to the contexts in which BFLA children are developing. The chapter (and the book) concludes by pointing out that BFLA children everywhere are able to understand and speak two languages from early on. Clearly, a bilingual learning context does not jeopardize the language development process but offers an opportunity that, unfortunately, monolingual children do not have access to.

Bilingual development: Good or bad?

When parents or teachers find out that I study bilingual children's language development, the first question I usually get is: 'and, what did you find, is it good for children or bad?'. I'm always a bit embarrassed when I get that question, since I really don't have an answer to it. One reason is that I disagree with one of the assumptions of the question, namely that bilingualism is somehow a choice (more about this in a bit). Another reason is that I'm not always sure what people mean by 'good' or 'bad' here. Of course, I do usually answer people's question and try to explain that it isn't my role to judge, but rather to find out in what circumstances a bilingual upbringing turns out well for all involved, and in what circumstances it might cause problems.

Back to the frequent assumption that a bilingual upbringing is a choice. It is true, future parents who as a couple know more than one language can very consciously decide whether or not to speak one or two languages to their children. Yet in many cases, there is no 'free' choice, since choosing against a bilingual upbringing for the children may imply cutting off part of the family from communicating with the new child, and the other way round (Lily, Arno, Ramon). Also, even when parents are proficient bilinguals, it may be emotionally hard or even impossible for them to speak to their newborn baby other than in the language they themselves were raised in (Xiu–Lily, Yun–Toshie).

Completely monolingual future parents who each speak just one and the same language have no choice as regards the language they will address their offspring in. Their single language is just the default. This is maybe why no one ever asks me whether monolingual acquisition is good. For many bilingual future parents, there isn't necessarily that much of a choice, either. The issue of 'good' or 'bad', then, doesn't seem to be very relevant – bilingual acquisition often is just the default.

Comparisons with monolinguals

The perceived special status of bilingual acquisition as the 'unusual' case for children to develop language skills is at the back of many people's minds, including those of parents in bilingual families. Implicit in many lay persons' and scholars' approaches to bilingual acquisition is the idea that bilingual children should resemble monolingual ones.

People who have been brought up bilingually often say of themselves that 'of course, I don't speak either of my languages as well as a monolingual', or, 'in school I was behind the monolingual children'. Others feel no such misgivings, and do not compare themselves to monolinguals.

One of the basic problematic issues with regard to how bilingually raised people regard themselves and how other people regard them lies in the constant comparison between bilingualism and monolingualism. Somehow, many people expect bilinguals to be two monolinguals in one – and not just any monolinguals, but monolinguals with highly advanced language skills.

Many people expect this also from children. They worry that bilingual input burdens children's minds, to the extent that children will have a delayed development, that is, in comparison to monolingual children. Many parents, schoolteachers and child health professionals believe that bilingual input can be a threat to children's development (Arno). As researchers, we can say time and again that comparisons with monolinguals are not necessary to understand the bilingual acquisition process, and that bilingual development should be studied in its own right, without reference to monolinguals. But that doesn't help bilingual families. They invariably meet up with the myth of bilingual input as a threat.

Researchers must address this fear, and compare bilinguals to monolinguals to see how they are doing. Also in this book I have drawn comparisons between bilingual and monolingual children in their language development. That's not because in fact BFLA *should* be compared to MFLA, or because MFLA should be seen as the standard. That's because it still needs to be proved to many people that child bilingualism does not 'hurt' a child or stand in the way of BFLA children's language development.

There is no intrinsic reason why bilinguals should be the same as monolinguals, just as there is no reason why monolinguals should be the same as bilinguals. However, the evidence to date and as discussed also in this book shows that, in fact, bilingual and monolingual children develop language in extraordinarily *similar* ways. Certainly, you find differences between a particular bilingual and monolingual child, but the magnitude of these differences is no greater than the range of variation there is between monolingual children among themselves, or bilingual children among themselves. Young MFLA children of the same age can differ widely in their level of proficiency in just one language, and so can BFLA children.

Variation in proficiency

The four BFLA children I followed in this book do not represent all bilingual children. Yet some of the variation among these four children reflects the major variation there is between BFLA children everywhere: one of the four children did not speak one of the languages (Toshie), another one used a lot of mixed utterances (Ramon) but two others hardly ever did (Lily, Arno), one developed both languages to a high degree (Arno), and another had very changing skills in each language (Lily).

What can explain these differences in proficiency between BFLA children, and the differences or similarities between their two languages? While the answers here are just starting to be investigated, there is increasing evidence that much depends on variations in the bilingual learning contexts.

Variation in bilingual learning contexts

Two of our four BFLA children had fairly steady bilingual input up until the age of six (Arno and Toshie). Both children's patterns of language use did not change much either: from the beginning of speech, Arno spoke both German and French with similar levels of proficiency, while Toshie pretty much only spoke Japanese (except for a few Korean words at the very start). The difference between Arno and Toshie couldn't be bigger, though: Arno spoke two languages, Toshie only one.

This matched two major differences between Arno's and Toshie's language learning contexts. First, Arno heard both German and French with equal frequency, and he heard a lot of each. In contrast, Toshie heard Korean much less often than she heard Japanese, simply because when she spent time with her mother, usually Japanese speakers were present, and so her mother spoke Japanese then. In Toshie's case, this also implied that the absolute amount of Korean she heard was very little, maybe on average only five hours per week or so. A second difference between Arno's and Toshie's bilingual environments is that Arno heard pretty much everyone in his environment speak both French and German to other people (including Arno). In speaking two languages himself, he was just doing what almost everybody around him did. In Toshie's case, she heard nobody speak Korean to her mother. Rather, Japanese was the only language she ever observed in conversations with the people around her. In just speaking Japanese herself, Toshie was also just doing what everybody around her did.

Lily used no mixed utterances, whereas Ramon used quite a few at some point. In Lily's environment, nobody used any mixed utterances. Ramon did hear mixed utterances regularly (grandma Rosa). Whether in Lily's language learning context anyone used specifically monolingual discourse strategies requiring Lily to use just unilingual utterances is not a relevant issue, since Lily said no mixed utterances that anyone could have reacted to. When Ramon said mixed utterances, his grandma Rosa used bilingual discourse strategies by not paying any special attention to them or even praising his use of English words.

Whereas Arno developed steadily in both languages, Lily sometimes developed both languages at the same rate, later increased developing in Language Alpha but stopped talking Language A, and even later greatly increased in her skill in Language A but stopped developing much in Language Alpha, only to again show increased skill in Language Alpha but no more use of Language A, and on and on.

In Arno's environment, both languages were continuously present every day. He experienced not a single day that he did not hear one of his languages. In contrast, Lily's language learning environment was characterized by highly changing input conditions for each language. In the Netherlands, she would hear far more Dutch than Mandarin, but she would hear both languages every day. In China, Lily heard no more Dutch for weeks on end.

These periods without Dutch occurred regularly, but not frequently (one trip a year). Lily's shifting language skills in each language closely mirrored the changes in her environment.

Whereas there are other aspects of BFLA children's language learning environments that can help explain some major aspects of their language use patterns and their skill in each language, the following factors are of major importance: the frequency with which BFLA children hear a particular language and changes in this frequency; the proportion of use of each language and changes in this proportion; the fact whether BFLA children hear a lot of mixed utterances or not; and the use of monolingual versus bilingual discourse strategies.

Parental work

Many parents are aware of the importance of the language contexts in which BFLA children learn to speak. For instance, Yun knew that she somehow had to make up for the low frequency with which Toshie heard Korean by reading books to her. Through book reading, Toshie could learn a lot of new words in a short time. Indeed, Yun's book reading with Toshie may be a major reason that Toshie continued to understand Korean, and was in fact later able to speak it when called upon at school. Similarly, through reading lots of Mandarin books with Lily, Xiu made sure that in the Netherlands Lily's Mandarin was not held back.

Other parents, like Alix and Bruno (Arno's mother and father) are not particularly aware of their important role as input providers, but may provide sufficient and supportive input anyhow.

Like Yun and later Julia (Ramon), parents may worry that they cannot succeed in raising their child to speak two languages. For parents like Yun it can be a big problem if things don't work out. For her, there was a lot of stress and effort involved in trying to get Toshie to speak Korean.

Indeed, making sure that children in a bilingual family become actively bilingual and speak two languages in acceptable ways may involve a great deal of work. The tips that 'help' publications for bilingual families offer are quite a lot of work to put into effect: for instance, getting videotapes in the two languages, seeking out playgroups where the minority language can be used, standing up to health professionals, family members and teachers who have a negative view of child bilingualism, teaching your child words in Language Alpha for words in Language A you never knew existed, reading books in two languages and so forth and so forth. And what if you don't succeed? The guilt can be overwhelming, and the sense of failure can cause family breakdown.

Similarly, Lanza (2007: 46) points out that 'many parents face problems as they attempt to raise their children bilingually. Many receive unfounded advice and lack the general support from any bilingual community, and hence abandon any attempts to establish individual bilingualism in the home [..] some of the important social repercussions of this failure include the inability of the child to communicate with grandparents and other family in the [..] homeland'.

Nevertheless, many bilingual parents do manage to raise bilingual children, even without a lot of extra work or feelings of inadequacy. However, they may be aided in this by the many publications that contain practical tips on how to raise bilingual children. At the end of this chapter, I have included a selection of some useful publications that fully take into account the latest research results.

In conclusion

With ever increasing mobility worldwide, there are more and more young couples consisting of partners from different linguistic and cultural backgrounds. The children born of these partnerships often grow up bilingually, meaning that they hear different people speak different languages on a pseudo-daily basis. These children have two first languages, A and Alpha.

In the last two decades, there has been a burgeoning of publications aimed at educating and supporting the parents in these bilingual families. Child bilingualism as fostered in bilingual families has also become an increasingly popular topic in the child language acquisition literature. The result of this research on young bilingual children's language development shows that, on the whole, they try to speak like the people acting as models for their two input languages. This is true for any language and any language combination that BFLA children are hearing around them. As such, there is no evidence for the pervasive myth that young bilingual children are confused and cannot get their languages straight. This unfounded myth unfortunately persists in large portions of society.

In this book, I have discussed examples from different languages and different language combinations, as if the particular languages do not matter. Also, the conclusions I have offered after each chapter make abstraction of the particular languages being learned. And, indeed, learning to distinguish between two languages in perception, understanding and producing translation equivalents, mostly using the 'right' language in the right circumstances, producing unilingual utterances that follow the rules of one particular language only, are all features that BFLA children share, irrespective of the particular languages they are acquiring.

Where it has been possible to make comparisons with monolingual acquisition, bilingual children have been found to develop their two languages in ways that are very similar to monolingual children. The important milestones of language development are reached at similar ages in monolingual and bilingual children alike. However, all too often, researchers in bilingual acquisition hold up monolingualism as a standard. Monolingual acquisition, though, is not the norm for bilingual acquisition, nor should it be. Bilingual acquisition can and needs to be studied in its own right. It is encouraging to see that established scholars in monolingual acquisition are emphasizing this as well.

As this book has shown, children can learn to understand and fluently speak two languages at a very early age. BFLA children can distinguish between their two languages in perception from the time they are born. By the time they are 10 months old, they understand words in each of their two languages. By the time they are 14 months old, some can already say the right words from the right language to a bilingual adult. By the time they are two years old, some can say sentences in each language that do not show any influence from the other language.

Clearly, then, young children are fully equipped to learn more than one language from early on. Yet there seem to be all sorts of processes that can interfere with a carefree learning of two languages from birth. What these processes consist of is finally starting to be investigated. For now, we can already identify a few factors that we know *support* the learning of any language: a warm, nurturing environment in which children are free to learn, and plenty of opportunities to hear and use whatever language or languages they are learning.

Activities and discussion points

1. Based on what you've learned in this book, and supposing the possibility arose for you to become part of a bilingual family as one of a child's parents, would you consider raising your child with two languages from birth? Why (not)? Have a class discussion about this.

2. Locate three websites in the language you know best (or, if you cannot find any, in another language you know) that discuss child bilingual development. Browse through those websites and rate them on whether in general you find the information on the website accurate and realistic judging from your understanding of this book. Explain why.

Further reading

Resources for parents and educators

Ada & Baker (2001), Baker (2007), Cunningham-Andersson & Andersson (2004), Harding-Esch & Riley (2008), Montanari (2002), Montanari *et al.* (2004), Pearson (2008)

Societal and environmental influences in BFLA

De Houwer (2009, Chapters 4 and 8), Pearson (2007)

Parental work in bilingual families

Lanza (2007), Okita (2002)

The emotional aspects of language use in bilingual families

De Houwer (2009, Chapter 8), Pavlenko (2004), Wong Fillmore (1991, 2000)

Glossary

- *Terms in the explanations that are themselves explained elsewhere in the glossary appear in bold face.*

- *As noted in the Preface, the explanations in this Glossary are only meant to facilitate the understanding of this book. Different linguists may place different emphases.*

1P/1L
A **language presentation** setting following the 'one person, one language' principle, where the important people (mostly the parents) in a child's **linguistic soundscape** each address the child using one language only.

1P/1L & 1P/2L
A **language presentation** setting in which some important people (including one parent) in a child's **linguistic soundscape** each address the child in two languages and in which other important people (including the other parent) address the child in one language only.

1P/2L
A **language presentation** setting in which the important people (mostly the parents) in a child's **linguistic soundscape** each address the child in two languages.

Articulatory organs
Parts of the body used for articulating speech sounds (e.g. lips and tongue).

Babble (babbling)
Infants' **production** of vowel–consonant combinations that sound like they could be **words**, but infants produce these without any apparent communicative meaning.

BFLA
See **Bilingual First Language Acquisition**.

BFLA children
Children who heard two languages spoken to them from birth.

Bilingual development
See **Bilingual First Language Acquisition**.

Bilingual discourse strategies
Meaning in this book: conversational habits that allow children to use two languages or mixed utterances.

Bilingual First Language Acquisition
The development of language in young children who heard two languages spoken to them from birth.

Clauses
Sentences that can be combined with others.

Cognates
Words that have the same **phonological** form and basic meaning across two languages.

Comprehension

The understanding of **words** and **sentences** in a language.

Dilingual conversation

Conversations in which one partner consistently speaks a different language than the other one. For this to be possible, both partners must understand the other one's language.

Early Second Language Acquisition

The situation where children first hear and learn one language (**Language 1**) from birth but where there is a change in children's language environments such that they start to hear and learn a second language after the first (**Language 2**).

Empirical research

Scientific research for which information has been systematically collected that can be used as evidence for a particular phenomenon.

ESLA

See *Early Second Language Acquisition.*

Holophrases

Early child **utterances** consisting of single **words** that appear to have much bigger meanings than the words by themselves have in adult usage.

IDS

See *Infant-Directed Speech.*

Infant-Directed Speech

The particular way of speaking many people use to address young children.

Infinitive

A verb form that does not agree in person or number with a subject and that is often used in a sentence together with a verb that does agree.

Interactions

Communicative settings in which people relate to each other face to face through verbal or non-verbal means.

Intonation patterns

Used in this book to refer to the overall 'melody' of an **utterance** or combination of syllables.

Language 1

A child's first or only input language (in **MFLA** and **ESLA**).

Language 2

A child's second input language (in **ESLA**).

Language A

One of a **BFLA** child's two first input languages.

Language Alpha

One of a **BFLA** child's two first input languages.

Language choice

The choice between languages that a bilingual person necessarily has to make when speaking and that results in the use of one particular kind of **utterance** rather than another (e.g. speaking French rather than Japanese, in the case of a person who can speak both French and Japanese).

Language presentation

Refers to who speaks which language(s) to a child and how many: one or two.

Linguistic soundscape

Meaning here: the totality of the various uses of spoken language that individuals encounter. This includes language use by people in one's social network, the media and overheard speech by people who are not part of one's social network.

Majority language

For a specific city or region, the main language used in public life.

Maturation

The process of physical, neurological and cognitive development that unfolds as babies grow older.

MFLA

*See **Monolingual First Language Acquisition**.*

Minority language

For a specific city or region, any language that is not used in public life.

Mixed utterances

Utterances with **words** or **morphemes** from two languages.

Monolingual discourse strategies

Meaning in this book: conversational habits that encourage children to speak only the language that their conversational partner is using.

Monolingual First Language Acquisition

The situation where children learn to understand and speak just one language, since they are hearing only one language (**Language 1**) from birth.

Morphemes

Grammatically or referentially meaningful parts of **words** (an entire word may consist of just one morpheme).

Overextension

The use of **words** in a way that includes much more than the common meaning, as in 'ball' to refer to any round object.

Phonemes

Single speech sounds that can make for changes of meaning in a particular language (e.g. the 'l' in 'lure' is a phoneme, since changing it to 's' as in 'sure' yields a different meaning).

Phonetically consistent forms

Fairly stable sounds that young children make and that apparently have some meaning for them but do not resemble adult words.

Phonological processes

Processes that from an adult point of view are used by children in attempting to produce speech segments and that involve mainly the deletion of particular **phonemes** or their substitution (compared to the adult form).

Production

Saying (producing) sounds, **words** or **sentences** that have meaning in a particular language.

Repairing (utterances)

Changing the form or content of utterances to make them better.

SDH

See **Separate Development Hypothesis**.

Sentences

It is impossible to formulate a definition of 'sentence' that all or even most linguists will agree on. I use the term 'sentence' in this book to refer to **utterances** containing at least a verb-like element. For sake of simplicity, I equate the notion sentence with that of 'clause'.

Separate Development Hypothesis

Children regularly exposed to two separate languages from birth develop two distinct grammatical systems.

Socialization

The process whereby people learn the cultural behaviors expected from them in the environments they live in.

Stronger language

The language that a BFLA child speaks best.

TEs

See **Translation equivalents**.

TFLA

See **Trilingual First Language Acquisition**.

Translation equivalents

Words that in the lives of young children adequately translate a word in the other language that children are hearing or speaking.

Trilingual First Language Acquisition

The learning of three languages in early childhood.

Underextension

The use of **words** in a way that is much more restricted than the regular meaning, for example, when a child says 'bus' only to the bus she takes with her mother to go shopping, but not to other buses.

Unilingual utterances

Utterances with **words** from one language only (both mono- and bilingual speakers can produce unilingual utterances).

Utterances

Speech sounds usually produced in one breath as part of a conversation or monologue, however short. Utterances can be **sentences** but they need not be (e.g. **babbling** 'baba' or saying 'yes' constitute utterances but not sentences; saying 'I'll do it' is an utterance that is also a sentence).

Weaker language

The language that a BFLA child speaks least well.

Words

It is impossible to really define what a word is. In this book I loosely define it as a part of language structure that typically you would find as an entry in a dictionary (since all the languages I am referring to have a written form, the question of what would happen for unwritten languages does not arise).

Bibliography

Ada, A.F. & Baker, C. (2001). *Guía para padres y maestros de niños bilingües.* (A guide for parents and teachers of bilingual children) Clevedon: Multilingual Matters (in Spanish).

Allen, S., Genesee, F., Fish, S. & Crago, M. (2002). Patterns of code mixing in English–Inuktitut bilinguals. In M. Andronis, C. Ball, H. Elston & S. Neuvel (eds), *Proceedings of the 37th Annual Meeting of the Chicago Linguistic Society (Vol. 2, pp. 171–188).* Chicago, IL: Chicago Linguistic Society.

Almgren, M. & Barreña, A. (2000). Bilingual acquisition and separation of linguistic codes: ergativity in Basque versus accusativity in Spanish. In K. Nelson, A. Aksu-Koç & C. Johnson (eds), *Children's language. Volume 11.* Mahwah, NJ: Lawrence Erlbaum Associates.

Álvarez, E. (1999). The role of language dominance in two narratives of a 7-year-old Spanish/English bilingual. *AILE (Acquisition et Interaction en Langue Etrangère), 1,* 83–95.

Álvarez, E. (2003). Character introduction in two languages: Its development in the stories of a Spanish–English bilingual child age 6;11–10;11. *Bilingualism: Language and Cognition, 6 (3),* 227–243.

Álvarez, E. (2008). The simultaneous development of narratives in English and Spanish. In C. Pérez-Vidal, M. Juan-Garau & A. Bel (eds), *A portrait of the young in the new multilingual Spain. Issues in the acquisition of two or more languages in multilingual environments* (pp. 159–182). Clevedon: Multilingual Matters.

Baker, C. (2007). *A parents' & teachers' guide to bilingualism (3rd revised edition).* Clevedon: Multilingual Matters.

Barnes, J.D. (2006). *Early trilingualism. A focus on questions.* Clevedon: Multilingual Matters.

Berman, R. (1979). The re-emergence of a bilingual: a case study of a Hebrew–English speaking child. *Working Papers on Bilingualism, 19,* 157–180.

Berman, R. (ed.) (2004). *Language development across childhood and adolescence.* Amsterdam/Philadephia: John Benjamins.

Bernardini, P. (2003). Child and adult acquisition of word order in the Italian DP. In N. Müller (ed.), *(In)vulnerable domains in multilingualism* (pp. 41–81). Amsterdam/Philadelphia: John Benjamins.

Bonnesen, M. (2008). On the 'vulnerability' of the left periphery in French/German balanced bilingual language acquisition. In P. Guijarro-Fuentes, M.P. Larrañaga & J. Clibbens (eds), *First language acquisition of morphology and syntax. Perspectives across languages and learners* (pp. 161–182). Amsterdam/Philadelphia: John Benjamins.

Bornstein, M.H. (2002). Parenting infants. In M.H. Bornstein (ed.), *Handbook of parenting Vol. 1 Children and parenting (2nd edition)* (pp. 3–43). Mahwah, NJ: Lawrence Erlbaum Associates.

Bornstein, M.H., Haynes, O.M. & Painter, K.M. (1998). Sources of child vocabulary competence: A multivariate model. *Journal of Child Language, 25,* 367–393.

Bornstein, M.H., Haynes, O.M., O'Reilly, A.W. & Painter, K.M. (1996). Solitary and collaborative pretense play in early childhood: Sources of individual variation in the development of representational competence. *Child Development, 67,* 2910–2929.

Bosch, L. & Sebastián-Gallés, N. (2001). Early language differentiation in bilingual infants. In J. Cenoz & F. Genesee (eds), *Trends in bilingual acquisition* (pp. 71–93). Amsterdam/Philadelphia: John Benjamins.

Brulard, I. & Carr, P. (2003). French–English bilingual acquisition of phonology: One production system or two? *International Journal of Bilingualism, 7(2)*, 177–202.

Cantone, K.F. (2007). *Code-switching in bilingual children*. Dordrecht: Springer.

Celce-Murcia, M. (1978). Phonological factors in vocabulary acquisition: a case study of a two-year-old, English–French bilingual. In E. Hatch (ed.), *Second language acquisition. A book of readings* (pp. 39–53). Rowley, MA: Newbury House.

Comeau, L. & Genesee, F. (2001). Bilingual children's repair strategies during dyadic communication. In J. Cenoz & F. Genesee (eds), *Trends in bilingual acquisition* (pp. 231–256). Amsterdam/Philadelphia: John Benjamins.

Comeau, L., Genesee, F. & Mendelson, M. (2007). Bilingual children's repairs of breakdowns in communication. *Journal of Child Language, 34*, 159–174.

Comeau, L., Genesee, F., Nicoladis, E. & Vrakas, G. (1997). Can young bilingual children identify their language choice as a cause of breakdown in communication? In E. Hughes, M. Hughes & A. Greenhill (eds), *Proceedings of the 21th Annual Boston University Conference on Language Development* (pp. 79–90). Somerville, MA: Cascadilla Press.

Conboy, B.T. & Thal, D. (2006). Ties between the lexicon and grammar: Cross-sectional and longitudinal studies of bilingual toddlers. *Child Development, 77*, 712–735.

Cruz-Ferreira, M. (2006). *Three is a crowd? Acquiring Portuguese in a trilingual environment*. Clevedon: Multilingual Matters.

Cunningham-Andersson, U. & Andersson, S. (2004). *Growing up with two languages. A practical guide (second edition)*. London: Routledge.

David, A. & Li, W. (2003). To what extent is code-switching dependent on a bilingual child's lexical development? *Sociolinguistica, 18*, 1–12.

David, A. & Li, W. (2005). The composition of the bilingual lexicon. In J. Cohen, K.T. McAlister, K. Rolstad & J. MacSwan (eds), *ISB4: Proceedings of the 4th International Symposium on Bilingualism* (pp. 594–607). Somerville, MA: Cascadilla Press.

David, A. & Li, W. (2008). Individual differences in the lexical development of French–English bilingual children. *International Journal of Bilingualism and Bilingual Education, 11*, 1–21.

De Houwer, A. (1990). *The acquisition of two languages from birth: A case study*. Cambridge: Cambridge University Press.

De Houwer, A. (1995). Alternance codique intra-phrastique chez des jeunes enfants bilingues. (the use of mixed utterances in young bilingual children) *AILE (Acquisition et Interaction en Langue Etrangère), 6*, 39–64.

De Houwer, A. (2005). Early bilingual acquisition: Focus on morphosyntax and the Separate Development Hypothesis. In J. Kroll & A. de Groot (eds), *The handbook of bilingualism* (pp. 30–48). Oxford: Oxford University Press.

De Houwer, A. (2007). Parental language input patterns and children's bilingual use. *Applied Psycholinguistics, 28(3)*, 411–424.

De Houwer, A. (2009). *Bilingual first language acquisition*. Clevedon: Multilingual Matters.

De Houwer, A., Bornstein, M.H. & De Coster, S. (2006). Early understanding of two words for the same thing: A CDI study of lexical comprehension in infant bilinguals. *International Journal of Bilingualism, 10(3)*, 331–347.

Deuchar, M. & Quay, S. (2000). *Bilingual acquisition: Theoretical implications of a case study*. Oxford: Oxford University Press.

Fenson, L., Dale, P., Reznick, S., Thal, D., Bates, E., Hartung, J., Pethick, S. & Reilly, J. (1993). *MacArthur Communicative Development Inventories: User's guide and technical manual*. San Diego, CA: Singular Publishing Group.

González-Bueno, M. (2005). Articulatory difficulties in the acquisiton of Spanish /r/ in a bilingual context. In J. Cohen, K.T. McAlister, K. Rolstad & J. MacSwan (eds), *ISB4: Proceedings of the 4th International Symposium on Bilingualism* (pp. 914–934). Somerville, MA: Cascadilla Press.

Goodz, N. (1989). Parental language mixing in bilingual families. *Infant Mental Health Journal, 10,* 25–44.

Gut, U. (2000a). *Bilingual acquisition of intonation: A study of children speaking German and English*. Tübingen: Max Niemeyer Verlag.

Gut, U. (2000b). Cross-linguistic structures in the acquisition of intonational phonology by German–English bilingual children. In S. Döpke (ed.), *Cross-linguistic structures in simultaneous bilingualism* (pp. 201–225). Amsterdam/Philadelphia: John Benjamins.

Harding-Esch, E. & Riley, P. (2008). *The bilingual family: A handbook for parents*. Cambridge: Cambridge University Press.

Hart, B. & Risley, T. (1995). *Meaningful differences in the everyday experiences of young American children*. Baltimore: Paul Brookes.

Holowka, S., Brosseau-Lapré, F. & Petitto, L.A. (2002). Semantic and conceptual knowledge underlying bilingual babies' first signs and words. *Language Learning, 52,* 205–262.

Hulk, A., & Müller, N. (2000). Bilingual first language acquisition at the interface between syntax and pragmatics. *Bilingualism: Language and Cognition, 3(3),* 227–244.

Ingram, D. (1981/82). The emerging phonological system of an Italian–English bilingual child. *Journal of Italian Linguistics, 2,* 95–113.

Jisa, H. (1995). L'utilisation du morphème *be* en anglais langue faible. (the use of the morpheme *be* in English, the weaker language) *AILE (Acquisition et Interaction en Langue Etrangère), 6,* 101–127.

Jisa, H. (2000). Language mixing in the weak language: Evidence from two children. *Journal of Pragmatics, 32,* 1363–1386.

Johnson, C. & Lancaster, P. (1998). The development of more than one phonology: A case study of a Norwegian–English bilingual child. *International Journal of Bilingualism, 2(3),* 265–300.

Johnson, C.E. & Wilson, I.L. (2002). Phonetic evidence for early language differentiation: Research issues and some preliminary data. *International Journal of Bilingualism, 6(3),* 271–289.

Juan-Garau, M. & Pérez-Vidal, C. (2000). Subject realization in the syntactic development of a bilingual child. *Bilingualism: Language and Cognition, 3,* 173–191.

Kehoe, M. (2002). Developing vowel systems as a window to bilingual phonology. *International Journal of Bilingualism, 6(3)*, 315–334.

Keshavarz, M.H. & Ingram, D. (2002). The early phonological development of a Farsi–English bilingual child. *International Journal of Bilingualism, 6(3)*, 255–269.

Kupisch, T. (2003). The DP, a vulnerable domain? Evidence from the acquisition of French. In N. Müller (ed.), *(In)vulnerable domains in multilingualism* (pp. 1–39). Amsterdam/Philadelphia: John Benjamins.

Lanvers, U. (1999). Lexical growth patterns in a bilingual infant: The occurrence and significance of equivalents in the bilingual lexicon. *International Journal of Bilingual Education and Bilingualism, 2*, 30–52.

Lanza, E. (1992). Can bilingual two-year-olds code-switch? *Journal of Child Language, 19*, 633–658.

Lanza, E. (1997). *Language mixing in infant bilingualism. A sociolinguistic perspective.* Oxford: Clarendon Press (see also the 2004 second, paperback edition with a new afterword published by Oxford University Press).

Lanza, E. (1998). Raising children bilingually in Norway. *International Journal of the Sociology of Language, 133*, 73–88.

Lanza, E. (2001). Temporality and language contact in narratives by children acquiring Norwegian and English simultaneously. In L. Verhoeven & S. Strömqvist (eds), *Narrative development in a multilingual context* (pp. 15–50). Amsterdam/ Philadelphia: John Benjamins.

Lanza, E. (2007). Multilingualism and the family. In P. Auer & Li Wei (eds), *Handbook of multilingualism and multilingual communication* (pp. 45–68). Berlin/New York: Mouton de Gruyter.

Leopold, W. (1970). *Speech development of a bilingual child. A linguist's record.* New York: AMS Press (original work published 1939–1949).

Lleó, C. & Rakow, M. (2005). Markedness effects in the acquisition of voiced stop spirantization by Spanish–German bilinguals. In J. Cohen, K.T. McAlister, K. Rolstad & J. MacSwan (eds), ISB4: *Proceedings of the 4th International Symposium on Bilingualism* (pp. 1353–1371). Somerville, MA: Cascadilla Press.

Lleó, C., Rakow, M. & Kehoe Winkler, M. (2007). Acquiring rhythmically different languages in a bilingual context. In J. Trouvain & W.J. Barry (eds), *Proceedings of the 16th International Congress of Phonetic Sciences* (pp. 1545–1548). Saarbrücken, Germany.

MacWhinney, B. (2000). *The CHILDES Project: Tools for analyzing talk (3rd edition).* Mahwah, NJ: Lawrence Erlbaum Associates.

Marchman, V.A., Martínez-Sussmann, C. & Dale, P.S. (2004). The language-specific nature of grammatical development: evidence from bilingual language learners. *Developmental Science, 7(2)*, 212–224.

Meisel, J. (1989). Early differentiation of languages in bilingual children. In K. Hyltenstam & L. Obler (eds), *Bilingualism across the lifespan. Aspects of acquisition, maturity and loss* (pp. 13–40). Cambridge: Cambridge University Press.

Meisel, J. (1990). INFL-ection: Subjects and subject-verb agreement. In J. Meisel (ed.), *Two first languages. Early grammatical development in bilingual children* (pp. 237–298), Dordrecht: Foris Publications.

Meisel, J. (2001). The simultaneous acquisition of two first languages. Early differentiation and subsequent development of grammars. In J. Cenoz & F. Genesee (eds), *Trends in bilingual acquisition* (pp. 11–41). Amsterdam/Philadelphia: John Benjamins.

Mishina, S. (1999). The role of parental input and discourse strategies in the early language mixing of a bilingual child. *Multilingua, 18,* 1–30.

Montanari, E. (2002). *Mit zwei Sprachen groß werden: Mehrsprachige Erziehung in Familie, Kindergarten und Schule.* (Growing up with two languages: multilingual child rearing in the family, preschool and school) München: Kösel (in German).

Montanari, E., Aarssen, J., Bos, P. & Wagenaar, E. (2004). Hoe kinderen meertalig opgroeien. (How children grow up multilingually) Amsterdam: PLanPlan (in Dutch).

Moon, C. & Fifer, W. (2000). Evidence of transnatal auditory learning. *Journal of Perinatology, 20,* S36–S43.

Müller, N. (1990). Developing two gender assignment systems simultaneously. In J. Meisel (ed.), *Two first languages. Early grammatical development in bilingual children* (pp. 193–236), Dordrecht: Foris Publications.

Müller, N., & Kupisch, T. (2003). Zum simultanen Erwerb des Deutschen und des Französischen bei (un)ausgeglichen bilingualen Kindern. *Vox Romanica, 62,* 145–169.

Nicoladis, E. (1998). First clues to the existence of two input languages: Pragmatic and lexical differentiation in a bilingual child. *Bilingualism: Language and Cognition, 1,* 105–116.

Nicoladis, E. (1999). 'Where is my brush-teeth?' Acquisition of compound nouns in a French–English bilingual child. *Bilingualism: Language and Cognition, 2,* 245–256.

Okita, T. (2002). *Invisible work. Bilingualism, language choice and childrearing in intermarried families.* Amsterdam/Philadelphia: John Benjamins.

Paradis, J. (2001). Are object omissions in Romance object clitic omissions? *Bilingualism: Language and Cognition, 4(1),* 36–37.

Paradis, J. & Genesee, F. (1996). Syntactic acquisition in bilingual children: autonomous or interdependent? *Studies in Second Language Acquisition, 18,* 1–25.

Paradis, J., Nicoladis, E. & Genesee, F. (2000). Early emergence of structural constraints on code-mixing: evidence from French–English bilingual children. *Bilingualism: Language and Cognition, 3(3),* 245–261.

Patterson, J. (1998). Expressive vocabulary development and word combinations of Spanish–English bilingual toddlers. *American Journal of Speech-Language Pathology, 7,* 46–56.

Patterson, J.L. (1999). What bilingual toddlers hear and say: Language input and word combinations. *Communication Disorders Quarterly, 21(1),* 32–38.

Patterson, J. (2000). Observed and reported expressive vocabulary and word combinations in bilingual toddlers. *Journal of Speech, Language and Hearing Research, 43,* 121–128.

Patterson, J.L. (2002). Relationships of expressive vocabulary to frequency of reading and television experience among bilingual toddlers. *Applied Psycholinguistics, 23(4),* 493–508.

Pavlenko, A. (2004). 'Stop doing that, ia komu skazala!': Emotions and language choice in bilingual families. *Journal of Multilingual and Multicultural Development, 25,* 179–203.

Pearson, B.Z. (2007). Social factors in childhood bilingualism in the United States. *Applied Psycholinguistics, 28,* 399–410.

Pearson, B.Z. (2008). Raising a bilingual child. A step-by-step guide for parents. New York: Living Language.

Pearson, B.Z. & Fernández, S. (1994). Patterns of interaction in the lexical development in two languages of bilingual infants. *Language Learning, 44,* 617–653.

Pearson, B.Z. & Navarro, A.M. (1996). Do early simultaneous bilinguals have a 'foreign accent' in one or both of their languages? In A. Aksu-Koç, E. Erguvanli-Taylan, A. Sumru Özsoy & A. Küntay (eds), *Perspectives on language acquisition: Selected papers from the VIIth International Congress for the Study of Child Language* (pp. 156–168). Istanbul: Bogaziçi University.

Pearson, B.Z., Fernández, S., Lewedeg, V. & Oller, D.K. (1997). The relation of input factors to lexical learning by bilingual infants. *Applied Psycholinguistics, 18,* 41–58.

Pearson, B.Z., Fernández, S., & Oller, D.K. (1993). Lexical development in bilingual infants and toddlers: comparison to monolingual norms. *Language Learning, 43,* 93–120.

Pearson, B.Z., Fernández, S., & Oller, D.K. (1995a). Cross-language synonyms in the lexicons of bilingual infants: one language or two? *Journal of Child Language, 22,* 345–368.

Pearson, B.Z., Navarro, A. & Gathercole, V.M. (1995b). Assessment of phonetic differentiation in bilingual learning infants. In D. MacLaughlin & S. McEwen (eds). *Proceedings of the 19th Annual Boston University Conference on Language Development* (pp. 427–438). Somerville, MA: Cascadilla Press.

Piller, I. (2002). *Bilingual couples' talk: The discursive construction of hybridity.* Amsterdam/Philadelphia: John Benjamins.

Porsché, D. (1983). *Die Zweisprachigkeit während des primären Spracherwerbs.* (Bilingualism in primary language acquisition) Tübingen: Gunter Narr Verlag.

Poulin-Dubois, D. & Goodz, N. (2001). Language differentiation in bilingual infants: Evidence from babbling. In J. Cenoz & F. Genesee (eds), *Trends in bilingual acquisition* (pp. 95–106). Amsterdam/Philadelphia: John Benjamins.

Qi, R. (2005). From nominal to pronominal person reference in the early language of a Mandarin–English bilingual child. In J. Cohen, K.T. McAlister, K. Rolstad & J. MacSwan (eds), *ISB4: Proceedings of the 4th International Symposium on Bilingualism* (pp. 1893–1909). Somerville, MA: Cascadilla Press.

Qi, R., di Biase, B. & Campbell, S. (2006). The transition from nominal to pronominal person reference in the early language of a Mandarin–English bilingual child. *International Journal of Bilingualism, 10(3),* 301–329.

Quay, S. (1995). The bilingual lexicon: Implications for studies of language choice. *Journal of Child Language, 22,* 369–387.

Radford, A., Kupisch, T., Köppe, R. & Azzaro, G. (2007). Concord, convergence and accommodation in bilingual children. *Bilingualism: Language and Cognition, 10,* 239–256.

Ronjat, J. (1913). *Le développement du langage observé chez un enfant bilingue.* (the development of language observed in a bilingual child) Paris: Champion.

Salustri, M. & Hyams, N. (2006). Looking for the universal core of the RI stage. In V. Torrens & L. Escobar (eds), *The acquisition of syntax in Romance languages* (pp. 159–182). Amsterdam/ Philadelphia: John Benjamins.

Saville-Troike, M. (1987). Dilingual discourse: the negotiation of meaning without a common code. *Linguistics, 25,* 81–106.

Schelletter, C. (2002). The effect of form similarity on bilingual children's lexical development. *Bilingualism: Language and Cognition, 5,* 93–107.

Schlyter, S. (1995). Formes verbales du passé dans des interactions en langue forte et en langue faible. (Past verb forms in interactions in the strong and the weak language) *AILE (Acquisition et Interaction en Langue Etrangère), 6,* 129–152.

Schlyter, S. (1996). Bilingual children's stories: French passé composé/imparfait and their correspondences in Swedish. *Linguistics, 34,* 1059–1085.

Schneider, R. (1999). L'expression des procès dans les récits d'un enfant bilingue. (The expression of process in the narratives of a bilingual child) *AILE (Acquisition et Interaction en Langue Etrangère), 1,* 63–82.

Schnitzer, M. & Krasinski, E. (1994). The development of segmental phonological production in a bilingual child. *Journal of Child Language, 21,* 585–622.

Schnitzer, M. & Krasinski, E. (1996). The development of segmental phonological production in a bilingual child: a contrasting second case. *Journal of Child Language, 23,* 547–571.

Serratrice, L. (2001). The emergence of verbal morphology and the lead-lag pattern issue in bilingual acquisition. In J. Cenoz & F. Genesee (eds), *Trends in bilingual acquisition* (pp. 43–70). Amsterdam/ Philadelphia: John Benjamins.

Serratrice, L. (2002). Overt subjects in English: evidence for the marking of person in an English–Italian bilingual child. *Journal of Child Language, 29 (2),* 1–29.

Serratrice, L. (2007). Referential cohesion in the narratives of bilingual English–Italian children and monolingual peers. *Journal of Pragmatics, 39,* 1058–1087.

Silva-Corvalán, C. (2003). Linguistic consequences of reduced input in bilingual first language acquisition. In S. Montrul & F. Ordóñez (eds), *Linguistic theory and language development in Hispanic languages* (pp. 375–397). Somerville, MA: Cascadilla Press.

Silva-Corvalán, C. & Sánchez-Walker, N. (2007). Subjects in early dual language development. A case study of a Spanish–English bilingual child. In K. Potowski & R. Cameron (eds), *Spanish in contact. Policy, social and linguistic inquiries* (pp. 3–22). Amsterdam/Philadelphia: John Benjamins.

Sinka, I. (2000). The search for cross-linguistic influences in the language of young Latvian–English bilinguals. In S. Döpke (ed.), *Cross-linguistic structures in simultaneous bilingualism* (pp. 149–174). Amsterdam/Philadelphia: John Benjamins.

Sinka, I. & Schelletter, C. (1998). Morphosyntactic development in bilingual children. *International Journal of Bilingualism, 2(3),* 301–326.

Swain, M. (1976). Bilingual first-language acquisition. In W. von Raffler-Engel & Y. Lebrun (eds), *Baby talk and infant speech* (pp. 277–280). Amsterdam: Swets & Zeitlinger.

van de Weijer, J. (1997). Language input to a prelingual infant. In A. Sorace, C. Heycock & R. Shillcock (eds). *Proceedings of the GALA '97 Conference on Language Acquisition* (pp. 290–293). Edinburgh, Scotland: University of Edinburgh.

Vila, I. (1984). Yo siempre hablo catalan y castellano: Datos de una investigacion en curso sobre la adquisicion del lenguaje en niños bilingües familiares. (I always speak Catalan and Spanish: Data from an on-going investigation into the acquisition of language in children growing up bilingually in the family) In M. Siguan (ed.), *Adquisición precoz de una segunda lengua* (Early acquisition of a second language) (pp. 31–51). Barcelona: Publicacions i Edicions de la Universitat de Barcelona.

von Raffler-Engel, W. (1965). Del bilinguismo infantile. (On infant bilingualism) *Archivio Glottologico Italiano, 50,* 175–180.

Wanner, P.J. (1996). A study of the initial codeswitching stage in the linguistic development of an English–Japanese bilingual child. *Japan Journal of Multilingualism and Multiculturalism, 2,* 20–40.

Werker, J.F. & Byers-Heinlein, K. (2008). Bilingualism in infancy: first steps in perception and comprehension of language. *Trends in Cognitive Sciences, 12(4),* 144–151.

Wölck, W. (1987/1988). Types of natural bilingual behavior: a review and revision. *The bilingual review/ La revista bilingüe, 14,* 3–16.

Wong Fillmore, L. (1991). When learning a second language means losing the first. *Early Childhood Research Quarterly, 6,* 232–346.

Wong Fillmore, L. (2000). Loss of family languages: Should educators be concerned? *Theory into Practice, 39(4),* 203–210.

Yamamoto, M. (2001). *Language use in interlingual families: A Japanese–English sociolinguistic study.* Clevedon: Multilingual Matters.

Index of the four BFLA children and their families

Subject index